DO ALL IN THE NAME OF THE LORD

DO ALL IN THE NAME OF THE LORD

A Festschrift for Mechelle Thompson

STAFF OF HERITAGE CHRISTIAN UNIVERSITY PRESS

Copyright © 2024 by Staff of Heritage Christian University Press

Cataloging-in-Publication Data

Do all in in the name of the Lord: a festschrift for Mechelle Thompson / by editors of Heritage Christian University Press.

p. cm. (Heritage Legacy Series).

Includes Scripture index.

ISBN 978-1-956811-49-0 (hbk); 978-1-956811-50-6 (ebook)

1. Bible—Criticism, interpretation, etc. 2. Evangelistic work. I. Thompson, Mechelle. II. Title. III. Series

081—dc20

Library of Congress Control Number: 2024931011

Cover design by Brad McKinnon and Brittany Vander Maas.

All rights reserved.

No part of this book may be reproduced in any form or by any electronic or mechanical means, including information storage and retrieval systems, without written permission from the author, except for the use of brief quotations in a book review.

Contents

Doing for the Lord	ix
Contributors	xiii
1. MARK 2:23–28 Coy D. Roper	1
2. JESUS: "HE WENT ABOUT DOING GOOD" Bill and Laura S. Bagents	26
3. THE SYROPHOENICIAN WOMAN Thomas Tidwell	39
4. DISRUPTIVE KINDNESS Travis Harmon	45
5. HERE I AM TO DO COMMUNITY OUTREACH Melissa McFerrin	57
6. REMEMBER WHO YOU ARE Dianne Tays	66
7. "A NEW COLLEGE WITH A NEW IDEA" Brad McKinnon	76
8. THE CALL OF WISDOM Lucas Suddreth	85
9. THE APOSTLE WHO LIVED Ed Gallagher	95
10. MATURITY IN MINISTRY Andrew Phillips	107
11. YOU CAN BE A LEADER, TOO Jamie Cox	117
12. THE NIGHT ETERNITY STOOD STILL Kirk Brothers	120

Scripture Index	127
Credits	135
Heritage Legacy Series	139
Also by Heritage Christian University Press	141
Heritage Christian University Press	143

Doing for the Lord

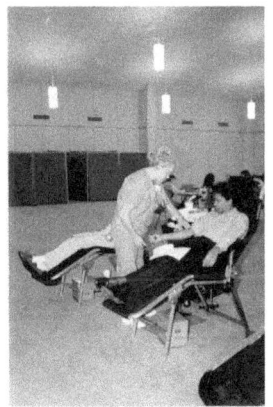

Contributors

Bill Bagents (DMin Amridge University) is Professor of Ministry, Counseling and Biblical Studies at Heritage Christian University, Florence, Alabama, USA.

Laura S. Bagents is a classroom teacher who has taught children's Bible classes in local congregations and adjunct courses at Heritage Christian University, Florence, Alabama, USA.

Kirk Brothers (PhD The Southern Baptist Theological Seminary) is President of Heritage Christian University, Florence, Alabama, USA.

Jamie Cox is librarian at Heritage Christian University, Florence, Alabama, USA.

Ed Gallagher (PhD Hebrew Union College) is Professor of Christian Scripture at Heritage Christian University, Florence, Alabama, USA.

Travis Harmon is Vice President of Student Services at Heritage Christian University, Florence, Alabama, USA.

Melissa McFerrin lives in Iron City, Tennessee, and is the Executive Assistant to the President at Heritage Christian University.

Brad McKinnon (PhD cand. University of Aberdeen) is Associate Professor of History at Heritage Christian University, Florence, Alabama, USA.

Andrew Phillips (PhD Regent University) is an Adjunct Instructor at Heritage Christian University, Florence, Alabama, USA. He has preached for the Graymere Church of Christ in Columbia, Tennessee since 2011.

Coy D. Roper (deceased in 2023) was a retired professor of Heritage Christian University, Florence, Alabama, USA.

Lucas Suddreth (M.Div., Harding School of Theology - Memphis) is the preacher at the Dublin-Powell church of Christ outside Columbus, OH. He has worked with congregations in Alabama, Tennessee, and Ohio. He also has a beautiful wife, Rachel, and two children, Sheppard and Marceline.

Dianne Tays retired in 2023 as the business office clerk at Heritage Christian University, Florence, Alabama, USA.

Thomas Tidwell (MA Heritage Christian University) is minister at South Cobb church of Christ.

Mark 2:23–28
JESUS, THE SABBATH, AND THE LAW
COY D. ROPER

In Mark 2:23–28 Jesus's disciples are accused of breaking the Law of Moses by plucking grain on the Sabbath.[1] Since Jesus's relationship to the Sabbath in particular and to the Law of Moses in general is one emphasis in this passage, it is possible that Mark 2:23–28 was intended to answer questions about the Law which might have troubled the early church, especially the church which Mark addressed.[2] In any case, the pericope suggests three questions concerning Jesus and the Law that need to be answered.

INTRODUCTION

However, before those questions can be addressed, some introductory matters need to be considered.

Text

There is one significant variant in the Markan passage. Some manuscripts omit the Greek words *epi Abiathar archiereos* which are translated "when Abiathar was high priest," and others add a genitive article which makes more acceptable the translation (as in the NIV) "in the days of Abiathar the high priest."[3] It is thought that the variants arose from the historical problem the text presents—namely, that Ahimelech, not Abiathar (Ahimelech's son), was the high priest who gave David the bread.[4] If the text as it is found is correct, there are several possible ways to explain the apparent contradiction between Jesus (or Mark) and 1 Samuel.[5] Lane suggests the possibility that the passage since it is similar in form to Mark 12:26, might be read "in the passage about Abiathar."[6]

Composition and Historicity

Various theories have been suggested concerning the formation of the pericope,[7] but in this paper, we will assume Mark has recorded an actual occurrence from the life of Jesus[8] as well as preserving Jesus's authentic words.

Author, Date, Audience

We will also assume that the author is John Mark, a companion of Paul and Barnabas (Acts 13:5) and the "son" (in the faith) of Peter (1 Pet 5:13); that, as early tradition indicates, he basically transmitted Peter's gospel; that he wrote the gospel in the late 50s or early 60s; and that it was intended for a congregation or group of congregations consisting largely of Gentile Christians (perhaps in Rome).[9]

Themes, Purpose

The major themes of Mark are Christology (emphasizing Christ's authority) in the first half of the book, and Discipleship (emphasizing service) in the second half.[10] Various suggestions have been made as to the purpose of the book, but the best possibilities relate to the goal of building up the church by teaching and encouraging Christians.[11]

How does Mark 2:23–28 contribute to the gospel's overall themes and purpose? The passage is the fourth of five "conflict" passages found between Mark 2:1 and Mark 3:6:

1. 2:1–12—Jesus accused of blasphemy because He forgave sins.
2. 2:13–17—Jesus accused of eating with tax collectors and sinners.
3. 2:18–22—Jesus asked why His disciples did not fast.
4. 2:23–28—Jesus asked why His disciples broke the Sabbath law.
5. 3:1–6—Jesus heals a man on the Sabbath, knowing that the Pharisees disapprove.

These conflicts culminate with the Pharisees conspiring with the Herodians to destroy Jesus (3:6). Mark has obviously brought several different conflict stories together[12] to set the course for the gospel he has written: This is a book which is about the Jesus who was crucified.[13] Emphasizing Jesus's death would encourage Mark's audience to continue to be faithful, no matter what, or, in other words, "to take up their cross and follow [Jesus]" (Mark 8:34).

In addition, these occurrences all speak of Jesus's relationship to the Law, emphasizing that in Jesus something new and different ("new wine" in "new wineskins," Mark 2:21–22) has come: one who can forgive sins (which was unheard of under the Law), one who eats with sinners (disregarding Pharisaic tradition), one whose disciples do not fast (unlike those who follow the Law and the traditions), and one who uses the Sabbath differently. The section reaches its climax when the Pharisees determine to seek Jesus's death—a decision brought about by Jesus's refusal to accept their interpretation of the Law. Thus, the passage may have a didactic purpose as well: to teach about Jesus's attitude towards the Law.

QUESTIONS ABOUT JESUS AND THE LAW

What does the passage teach about Jesus and the Law? The answer lies in three questions related to the text.

Mark 2:23–24—Did Either Jesus or His Disciples Break the Law?

Jesus and His disciples were going through a grain field on the Sabbath; the disciples "began to pluck heads of grain" (Matthew says that they ate the grain [Matt 12:1], and Luke adds that "they rubbed them in their hands, and ate them" [Luke 6:1]); and the Pharisees accused them of doing what was not lawful on the Sabbath (2:23–24). They did not accuse Jesus of breaking the law; it seems likely that if they could have done so, they would have.[14] Still, since the accused were His disciples, Jesus was held accountable for their actions.[15]

What law did they break? The Old Testament explicitly allowed for those passing through a field to gather and eat from the fruit of the field (see Deut 23:25). They could not, therefore, be accused of stealing.[16]

Rather, the Pharisees accused the disciples of breaking the law against working on the Sabbath (Exod 20:8-11), in particular the law that required keeping the Sabbath even during harvest times (Exod 34:21). The Jews had elaborated the Sabbath law to include thirty-nine categories of work which could not be done; among those categories was "reaping."[17] The "law" which the Pharisees accused the disciples of breaking consisted of their traditions.

But was this really the equivalent of breaking the Law of Moses?[18] Jesus Himself distinguished between the Pharisees' traditions and Moses's law. When the disciples were accused of eating with unwashed hands, Jesus replied: "You abandon the commandment of God and hold to human tradition" (Mark 7:8; see also Matt 15:3–6). "The commandment of God" here is the command to "honor your father and your mother" (Mark 7:10), one of the Ten Commandments. Thus, Jesus demonstrated the utmost respect for the Law of Moses, but little respect for the traditions of the elders.[19]

It seems clear, then, that Jesus did not at this time break the Law of Moses,[20] nor did His disciples.[21] The assertion that Jesus's failure to deny His opponents' accusation means that He accepted it[22] is not valid, since, according to Matthew, Jesus makes it clear that the disciples were "guiltless" (Matt 12:8). If they were guiltless, they had not broken the Sabbath.

One further point needs to be made: there is a theological problem if Jesus did indeed break the Law of Moses. Jesus was a Jew who lived under the Law (Gal 4:4); as a Jew, He had the responsibility to obey the Law (Exod 19:5). If He failed to obey it, then He sinned (Jas 2:10). However, the New Testament teaches, and followers of Christ believe, that Jesus did not sin.[23] Therefore, Jesus never broke God"s law. To say that on this occasion He broke the law requires a revision of New Testament theology or some kind of explanation to show how Jesus could break the law and still be sinless.

Mark 2:25–27—Did Jesus Approve of the Breaking of the Law?

Jesus replies to the Pharisees' accusation by citing David's eating of the bread of the Presence, which, He said, "was not lawful for any but the priests to eat" (2:26). Then He adds the saying, "The Sabbath was made for [man], not [man] for the Sabbath." In using David's example, He seems to endorse what He Himself calls unlawful.

The law David broke is found in Leviticus 24:8–9, which specifies that the priests are to eat the loaves in a holy place. On the occasion Jesus cited (as recorded in 1 Sam 21:1–6), David asked for bread for himself and his men. The priest Ahimelech said that he had none except for the holy bread, which David could have, "provided the young men have kept themselves from women." When David said they had, "the priest gave him the holy bread; for there was no bread there except the bread of the Presence." Although both Matthew and Luke say that David "entered the house of God," Jesus calls attention only to the eating of the bread.[24]

The usual (but not universal) interpretation of Mark 2:25–26 is that Jesus uses David's precedent to prove that meeting human needs is more important than observing sabbath details.[25] Just as David and his companions were "hungry and in need of food," Jesus's disciples were hungry (a fact which is specified by Matthew). To rebuke them for taking sustenance was altogether out of place, especially since "the Sabbath was made for [man], and not [man] for the Sabbath." The Sabbath law was given as a blessing for humanity; when it was used to keep the poor from eating, then its purpose was perverted. A similar argument is used by Jesus when He asks the Pharisees in the next chapter: "Is it lawful to do good on the Sabbath or to do harm, to save life or to kill?" (Mark 3:4) The implied argument is that since the Sabbath is intended to be a blessing to man, it is always appropriate to do good on the Sabbath.

Does this mean that Jesus endorsed the breaking of the Law of Moses? Not necessarily. There are two ways to argue that, although Jesus appears to endorse David's breaking of the law, in reality, He did not.

A higher law. It is possible to see in this incident Jesus's endorsement of the principle that some Old Testament laws are more important than others, and when two laws seem to come into conflict, the higher law takes precedence.

That Jesus considered some laws more important is demonstrable. He spoke of the two greatest commandments (Mark 12:28–34), implying that there was a hierarchy of laws. In Matthew 23:23, He said the law's requirements of justice, mercy, and faith were more important than tithing garden vegetables, even though the less important things should still be done. In this, He followed the Old Testament prophets. Micah said the Lord desires, not burnt offerings, but "to do justice, and to love kindness, and to walk humbly with God ... ."[26]

Matthew adds that Jesus said, "If you had known what this means, 'I desire mercy and not sacrifice,' you would not have condemned the guiltless." (Matt 12:7) Jesus quotes from Hosea 6:6, applying the passage to His accusers. They lacked "mercy"—for the hungry disciples—even though they were concerned about "sacrifice"—the keeping of the Sabbath—and thus they had given more prominence to a less important law and neglected another law that was more important.

One could therefore conclude that Jesus uses David as an example not to prove that it is all right to break the law, but to demonstrate that in certain circumstances one law may take precedence over another. David did break one law, but was excused because he was obedient to a higher law. Likewise, if the disciples had broken the Sabbath law, they should be excused because they were obedient to a higher law: the right to eat in order to survive if survival requires no more than breaking a law relating to ritual.[27]

An ad hominem argument. A second possibility is that Jesus was using an *ad hominem* argument. Clark defined the *ad hominem* argument as

> a form of argument that accepts the propositions accepted by another for the purpose of deducing contra-

dictory propositions or propositions that would be rejected by the other person from them.[28]

If Jesus was using this kind of argument, He cited David's example as one of which the Pharisees approved without expressing His own approval, saying something like this: "David broke the law, and you approve of what David did. What these men have done is not as obviously a breach of the law as David's action. Why then do you condemn them?"[29] In such a case, Jesus does not necessarily say that He agrees with their view that what David did was right, but accuses them of inconsistency in their criticism of His disciples.

Jesus apparently uses the same kind of reasoning when He says to the Pharisees, "Those who are well have no need of a physician, but those who are sick; I have come to call not the righteous but sinners" (Mark 2:17; see also Matt 9:12–13; Luke 5:31–32; and compare Luke 7:36–50). It is unlikely that He Himself endorses the view that the Pharisees were "well" or "righteous" (see Matt 23); rather he speaks of their own view of themselves. Jesus may be saying something like: "Granting for the moment that you are what you think you are—namely righteous—, you should understand why I associate with sinners, and you should be glad that I do."[30] If He uses this kind of argument regarding eating with sinners, it may also be the kind of argument He uses in the controversy regarding the Sabbath. It may be possible to find *ad hominem* arguments elsewhere in the New Testament as well.[31]

Emphasis. In either case, Jesus's answer focuses on two facts:

1. *David's action.* It is probable that the Pharisees would have been unwilling to regard as acceptable such behavior from anyone else. The fact that it was David who provided the precedent for the disciples' action is important: it lays the foundation for David's son Jesus to claim authority.
2. *Human needs.* In the conflict stories, Jesus demonstrates that He is sensitive to human needs, but His critics are not: He heals, eats with sinners, and defends the hungry. Only in the case of the question about fasting is "human need" not a major factor in the story, but even there it may play a part: Jesus does not force people to deny themselves food.

Mark 2:28—How then does Jesus relate to the Law of Moses?

After Jesus has defended Himself by citing David's example and by declaring that the "Sabbath was made for [man]," He announces, "So the Son of Man is lord even of the Sabbath." The expression "Son of Man" is Jesus's favorite designation for Himself; it speaks, not just of His humanity, but of His identification with the "Son of Man" in Daniel 7:13; thus, it includes a reference to His divinity.[32] When Jesus says that the "Son of Man" is "lord even of the Sabbath," He claims the right to rule over the Sabbath. And if He is "lord of the Sabbath," then He has the right, if He chooses, to break (or abrogate or alter) the law of the Sabbath.[33] The Pharisees, therefore, have no right to criticize His use of the Sabbath.

While this is clear enough, the link between this saying

and what precedes it is not so clear. The English (NRSV) text has "The Sabbath was made for [man], and not [man] for the Sabbath; so the Son of Man is lord even of the Sabbath." It is hard to see how the "so" in the second clause relates to what has gone before.

The Greek word that connects the two clauses is *hoste*. Arndt-Gingrich defines this use as meaning "for this reason, therefore, so" and gives eighteen New Testament examples, including Mark 2:28.[34] In most of these cases, the logical connection between the *hoste* clause and the preceding is obvious. For example, after pointing out that his listeners will save a sheep on the Sabbath, Jesus in Matthew 12:12 says, "How much more valuable is a human being than a sheep! So (*hoste*) it is lawful to do good on the Sabbath."[35] But the same kind of logical connection is harder to see in Mark 2:28.

Probably the connection lies in the fact that in many cases in the New Testament, the independent clause following *hoste* contains an important general truth that follows from one or more specific cases or arguments. This is true of Matthew 12:12: the *hoste* clause states the general principle "it is lawful to do good on the Sabbath." Matthew 19:6 provides another example: "So (*hoste*) they are no longer two, but one flesh."[36] Mark 2:28 fits this pattern; Mark 2:27 provides a specific fact which is then used to lead into an important general truth. The connection between the two verses lies in the use of "man" (NRSV: humankind; Greek: *anthropon*) in 2:27 and "Son of Man" (*huios tou anthropou*) in 2:28. The argument is that if the Sabbath was made for man, then man is superior to the Sabbath. But if man is superior to the Sabbath, how much more can the same be said of the one who shares manhood, but is more than man, the Son of Man! Thus, since the Sabbath was made for man, the Son of Man is lord of the Sabbath![37]

But if Jesus is "lord of the Sabbath," He is also "lord of the Law," for the Sabbath law was especially important to the Jews during the New Testament era. For the readers of Mark's gospel, this fact, coming as it does near the end of several conflicts that relate to the Law, would have been meaningful for all those conflicts. If there are conflicts concerning the Law in the church(es) for which Mark writes, recognition of Jesus's lordship over the Law would be an important factor in resolving those conflicts.

In addition, Jesus's lordship places Him in a position of great authority, an emphasis in the conflict stories.[38] Besides His claim to authority over the Sabbath, He claims to have authority to forgive sins (2:10). Furthermore, His call of Levi (2:14), His designation of Himself as a "physician" (2:17) and as the "bridegroom" (2:19), and His defiant stance in healing on the Sabbath (3:3–5) all suggest that He claimed authority. Perhaps most telling would have been the "new wine" metaphor (2:21–22) in which He apparently was claiming the right to institute something new in religion, which was unlike Judaism and unlike the Law. Jesus's insistence on His authority coincides with the emphasis in the first half of the book of Mark, and provides the basis for the Jews' plot to kill Him.[39]

CONCLUSION

In this passage, Jesus demonstrates that His opponents are inconsistent in their application of the Law, ignorant of its true meaning, insensitive to human needs, and insubordinate to the Son of Man who is lord of the Law.

While the passage does not indicate that Jesus or his disciples broke the Law of Moses, it does demonstrate that they did not consider themselves bound to keep the traditions of the Jews. It may also suggest that under the Law some laws took precedence over others; in particular, laws which related to meeting human needs were more important than laws relating to ritual. Above all, it proclaims the fact that Christ is lord of the Law; He is its maker and ruler; He can break it if He chooses; the fact that He chose to keep it was an act of grace.

Some applications of this passage are suspect. It has been used to teach how the "Christian Sabbath" (the Lord's Day) should be kept.[40] Since the Law has been taken away, such an application is inappropriate. Also inappropriate is Collier's suggestion that Matthew's version of this passage demonstrates that "the deeper concerns of God's heart are more important than the specific instructions of God's law (which also is important)" and that in it "Jesus shows that the real issues of Biblical hermeneutics go beyond being focused on the text, to a focus on the heart of God as it reaches out to people."[41]

Since in this passage, the disciples obey the "specific instructions of God's law," and since the "desires of God's heart" are found in specific texts, Collier's suggestion is unclear or unnecessary or dangerous (since it might lead one deliberately to ignore Biblical teaching).

Perhaps the best application is simply to take note of:

1. Jesus's respect for the Law under which He lived, contrasted with His apparent disdain for Jewish traditions.
2. Jesus's concern for the needs of people, is contrasted with the lack of concern of His opponents.
3. Jesus's authority, which led Him ultimately to deliver a new covenant, under which His disciples are privileged and obligated to live.

ENDNOTES

[1.] Parallels are found in Matthew 12:1–8 and Luke 6:1–5.

[2.] Questions about the Law and its relationship to Christians were common among New Testament congregations. In fact, the church at Rome, which is often thought to be the original recipient of the gospel of Mark (see below), was troubled by such issues. Dunn believes that the stories in this section of Mark were brought together because they all relate to controversies concerning the Law—and to aspects of the Law that were regarded as crucial by the Jews: table fellowship (involving rules related to clean and unclean foods), fasting, and Sabbath-keeping. See James D. G. Dunn, "Mark 2.1–3.6: A Bridge Between Jesus and Paul on the Question of the Law," *New Testament Studies* 30 (1984): 401.

3. Notes, *Greek New Testament*, United Bible Societies, 3rd edition.

4. Bruce M. Metzger, *A Textual Commentary on the Greek New Testament* (New York: United Bible Societies, 1971), 79; William L. Lane, *The Gospel According to Mark* (Grand Rapids, MI: Eerdmans, 1974), 115–116.

5. See M. R. Mulholland, "Abiathar," *Dictionary of Jesus and the Gospels*, eds. Joel B. Green, Scot McKnight, and I. Howard Marshall (Downers Grove, IL: InterVarsity Press,1992), 524 (hereafter abbreviated as *DJG*), 1–2; William Hendriksen, *New Testament Commentary—Exposition of the Gospel According to Mark* (Grand Rapids, MI: Baker, 1975), 106–108; Gleason L. Archer, *Encyclopedia of Bible Difficulties* (Grand Rapids, MI: Zondervan, 1982), 362.

6. Lane, 116.

7. For various views of the development of the pericope, and its historicity (or lack of historicity), see F. W. Beare, "The Sabbath Was Made for Man," *Journal of Biblical Literature* 79 (1960): 130–136; Arland J. Hultgren, "The Formation of the Sabbath Pericope in Mark 2:23–28," *Journal of Biblical Literature* 91 (March 1972): 38–43; Maurice Casey, "Culture and Historicity: The Plucking of the Grain (Mark 2.23–28)," *New Testament Studies* 34 (1988): 1–23. Lane (pp. 117, 118) notes the difficulties in the text but says that v. 27 is an "authentic pronouncement of Jesus" (p. 119), adding, however, that he believes that v. 28 is Mark's editorial comment (p. 120)—a view accepted by C. E. B. Cranfield, *The Gospel According to St. Mark,* The Cambridge Greek New Testament Commentary, ed. C. F. D. Maule (Cambridge: University Press, 1972), 118; and by Walter W. Wessel, "Mark," in The Expositor's Bible Commentary.

gen. ed. Frank E. Gaebelein, vol. 8 (Grand Rapids, MI: Zondervan, 1984), 638.

8. Contrary to the opinion of Schweizer, who says that "this story appears to be fictitious." Eduard Schweizer, *The Good News According to Mark*. trans. Donald H. Madvig (Atlanta: John Knox Press, 1970).

9. Class notes, The Gospel of Mark, Harding University Graduate School of Religion, Memphis, TN, instructor Allen Black, Spring 1995. See also Lane, 1–32, and D. A. Carson, Douglas J. Moo, and Leon Morris, *An Introduction to the New Testament* (Grand Rapids, MI: Zondervan, 1992), 89–109.

10. Class notes.

11. Class notes. See also R. A. Guelich, "Mark, Gospel of," *DJG*, 524.

12. After the first narrative, there are no time markers to indicate that the events happened one after the other.

13. Finding these stories with this conclusion so early in the book gives credence to the oft-quoted statement that Mark "is a passion-narrative with an extended introduction." (Lane, 2, quoting Martin Kahler.)

14. See R. A. Cole, *The Gospel According to St. Mark*. The Tyndale New Testament Commentaries (Grand Rapids, MI: Eerdmans, 1961), 72.

15. Lane, 115.

16. Neither is there evidence that the disciples were accused of disregarding traditional restrictions on sabbath travel. (A fact Schweizer [p. 70] comments on.)

17. Lane, 114–115; Royce Gordon Gruenler, "Mark," in *Evangelical Commentary on the Bible*. ed. Walter A. Elwell, (Grand Rapids, MI: Baker Book House, 1989), 6.

18. Some commentators state flatly that Jesus or the disciples broke the Law. See John R. Donahue, "Mark," *Harper's Bible Commentary,* gen. ed. James L. Mays (San Francisco, Harper, 1988), 988.

19. See Matthew 5:17-20. (Although Jesus apparently voluntarily keeps some of the traditions. D. J. Moo, "Law," *DJG*, 452.) It is in this light that we should understand Matthew 23:2: Jesus taught that *as long as* the scribes and Pharisees teach what Moses taught, follow their teachings.

20. Furthermore, evidence is absent that Jesus ever broke the Law of Moses. See Moo, 451-452, 455.

21. See: James Burton Coffman, *Commentary on Mark* (Austin, Texas: Finn Foundation Publishing House, 1975), 50; C. E. W. Dorris, *A Commentary on the Gospel by Mark* (Nashville, TN: Gospel Advocate Company, 1950), 65.

22. Some writers assume from silence that Jesus accepted the charge of law-breaking. See Wessel, 638; Dorris, 68.

23. See: 2 Corinthians 5:21; Hebrews 4:15; 7:26; 1 Peter 2:22; 3:18; James 5:6; 1 John 3:5. "The teaching that Jesus Christ was sinless (impeccable) ... has been a universal conviction of the Christian church." M. E. Osterhaven, "Sinlessness of Christ," *Evangelical Dictionary of Theology.* ed. Walter A. Elwell (Grand Rapids, MI: Baker, 1984, 1990), 1018.

24. There is no indication that David ate in the house of God. Nor is there any evidence that David's action occurred on the Sabbath, although that was believed by the Jews.

25. Hicks, writing of the incident as recorded in Matthew, says, "The issue is whether human need overrides

a ceremonial law such as consecrated bread on the Sabbath." John Mark Hicks, "The Sabbath Controversy in Matthew: An Exegesis of Matthew 12:1–14," *Restoration Quarterly* 27 (1984), 84. See: Schweizer, 72; Dorris, 65ff.; Enos Dowling, R. C. Foster, Frank H. Marshall, and Orrin Root, *Mark*. Standard Bible Commentary, ed. Kenton K. Smith (Cincinnati, OH: Standard Publishing, 1968), 19, 20; Gruenler, 771; Matthew Henry, *A Commentary on the Holy Bible,* volume 5 of 6 (London: Marshall Brothers, Ltd., n.d.), 266; E. Bickersteth and J. R. Thomson, "St. Mark," *The Pulpit Commentary,* ed. H. D. M. Spence and Josephs. Exell, volume 16 (Grand Rapids, MI: Eerdmans, 1950 reprint), 88; Earle McMillan, *The Gospel According to Mark* (Austin, TX: Sweet Publishing Company, 1973), 43; William Barclay, *The Gospel of Mark* (Philadelphia: The Westminster Press, 1954, 1956), 58; Cole, 73; Joseph A Fitzmyer and Raymond E. Brown (eds.), *The Jerome Biblical Commentary*, volume 2: The New Testament and Topical Articles (Englewood Cliffs, NJ: Prentice-Hall, Inc., 1968), 27. Among commentators who dispute the idea that Jesus taught that "need" or "necessity" allowed one to break the Law are: Cranfield, 115; Coffman, 104; J. W. McGarvey and Philip Y. Pendleton, *The Fourfold Gospel* (Cincinnati, OH: The Standard Publishing Company, n. d.), 211.

26. Micah 6:6–8. Probably Micah's words should be understood as meaning that God is not pleased with sacrifices *alone,* without righteous living.

27. This is the way many commentators understand the passage. Wessel (638) quotes Ralph Earle, *The Gospel According to Mark*, The Evangelical Commentary on the Bible (Grand Rapids: Zondervan, 1957), 49: "Human need

is a higher law than religious ritualism." See also: Gruenler, 770, 771; Cole, 73; Barclay, 58; McMillan, 43. This is apparently the way Alexander Campbell, *The Christian System* (Cincinnati, OH: Standard Publishing Company, n.d.), 72 viewed this passage, although his terminology is different (and difficult).

[28.] Clark differentiates between the *ad hominem* argument and the "*abusive ad hominem*, a logical fallacy in which irrelevancies of character are used as reasons for rejecting a position." Gordon H. Clark, *Logic* (Jefferson, MD: The Trinity Foundation, 1985, 1988), 133. Most modern books on logic and argumentation deal only with *ad hominem* as a fallacy in which one attacks one's opponent's character instead of dealing with his or her arguments. See, for example, W. Ward Fearnside and William B. Holther, *Fallacy—The Counterfeit of Argument* (Englewood Cliffs, NJ: Prentice-Hall, 1959), 99–101, and Patrick J. Hurley, *A Concise Introduction to Logic* (Belmont, CA: Wadsworth Publishing Company, 1982), 75–76. Apparently, in the nineteenth century, the *ad hominem* argument as defined by Clark was well established. It is cited as a legitimate kind of argument by James D. Bales in *Christian, Contend for Thy Cause,* (Searcy, AR: Bales' Book Club, n. d), 131, in which he uses an 1893 book, *Elements of Deductive Logic,* to define the argument; and it is recommended as a method of indirect refutation by John A. Broadus in the book *On the Preparation and Delivery of Sermons* which was originally published in 1870 (new and revised edition by Jesse Burton Weatherspoon; New York: Harper & Row, 1944), 188–189.

[29.] "Jesus did not say whether David's act was right or wrong, but it is clear that the critical Pharisees considered it at least allowable. Since they did not criticize David for breaking the law to satisfy his hunger, why did they criticize Jesus' disciples?" Dowling, et al., 19.

30. Lane (105) says one possibility is that "'righteous' is used ironically or *ad hominem,* while the 'sinners' are the humble who hear and respond to the call of God." Other commentators take the "righteous" to mean the "self-righteous." See, for example, Wessel, 635.

31. Broadus (188–189) cites Matthew 12:27 and 1 Corinthians 15:29 as examples of *ad hominem* arguments. G. C. Brewer uses Matthew 12:22–30 (and parallels) and Matthew 12:1–8 (with Mark 2:23–28) as examples. *Contending for the Faith* (Nashville, TN: Gospel Advocate Company, 1955), 239–247.

32. The meaning of the expression "Son of Man" is a much-discussed issue. For a comprehensive survey of various views, see I. H. Marshall, "Son of Man," *DJG,* 775–781.

33. See: Cole, 74; McMillan, 44; Wessel, 638; Dorris, 68; Dowling, et al., 20.

34. William F. Arndt and F. Wilbur Gingrich, *A Greek-English Lexicon of the New Testament and Other Early Christian Literature* (Chicago: The University of Chicago Press, 1957), 908. The usage referred to is the introduction of independent clauses followed by the indicative. The examples are: Matthew 12:12; 19:6; 23:31; Mark 2:28; 10:8; Roman 7:4, 12; 13:2; 1 Corinthians 3:7; 7:38; 11:27; 14:22; 2 Corinthians 4:12; 5:16f; Gal 3:9, 24; 4:7, 16. Moule indicates that *hoste* "is also, in certain contexts, simply an inferential particle as if *hoste,* meaning, and so, accordingly, etc." and then gives many of the same examples. C. F. D. Moule, *Idiom Book of New Testa-*

ment Greek, 2nd ed. (New York: Cambridge University Press, 1953, 1959), 144.

35. The idea is: "Since (*hoste*) you will help a sheep on the sabbath, it is lawful to do good on the sabbath—and even more so to do good to a human being!"

36. For the same pattern, see also Romans 7:12; 3:12; 1 Corinthians 3:7; 7:38; 11:27; 14:22; Galatians 3:9; et al.

37. What would Jesus's hearers have understood? The repetition of *anthropos* probably would have been ambiguous, since "son of man" can simply mean "man." Many probably went away wondering what Jesus had meant. This in turn suggests that the "Messianic secret" probably remained a secret from most even after this revelation from Jesus.

38. "In all five the principal issue seems to be the authority claimed by Jesus, implicitly or explicitly ..." Dunn, 397, 398.

39. Sigal says that Jesus did no more than any other "proto-rabbi" of his time. His views differed from the views of the Pharisees, but so did the views of others like Him. He claimed authority to set aside the Halakah of others and publish His own, but so did others. In giving primacy to the love command and stressing "mercy and not sacrifice," He did no more than other proto rabbinic figures. He consistently expressed His authoritative teachings in proto-rabbinic style and form. Philip Sigal, *Judaism: The Evolution of a Faith* (Grand Rapids, MI: Eerdmans, 1988), 73–76. Sigal provides a valuable corrective to the danger of placing too great an emphasis on the ways in which Jesus differed from the Jews. Nevertheless, one should keep in

mind that the differences were sufficient to result in Jesus's crucifixion.

[40.] As is done by earlier commentators. See: Henry, 266; *Pulpit Commentary,* 89; G. A. Chadwick, *The Gospel According to St. Mark,* The Expositor's Bible, ed. W. Robertson Nicoll (London: Hodder and Stoughton, 1893), 69.

[41.] Gary D. Collier, "An Assessment of the Hermeneutical Impasse in Churches of Christ," Part 2, *Christian Scholars Conference,* 1988, 27.

WORKS CITED

Archer, Gleason L. *Encyclopedia of Bible Difficulties.* Grand Rapids, MI: Zondervan, 1982.

Arndt, William F., and F. Wilbur Gingrich. *A Greek-English Lexicon of the New Testament and Other Early Christian Literature.* Chicago: University of Chicago Press, 1957.

Bales, James D. *Christian, Contend for Thy Cause.* Searcy, AR: Bales' Book Club, n. d.

Barclay, William. *The Gospel of Mark.* Philadelphia: Westminster Press, 1954, 1956.

Beare, F. W. Beare. "The Sabbath Was Made for Man." *Journal of Biblical Literature* 79 (1960): 130–136.

Bickersteth, E., and J. R. Thomson. "St. Mark." *The Pulpit Commentary.* eds. H. D. M. Spence and Joseph S. Exell. vol. 16. Grand Rapids, MI: Eerdmans, 1950 reprint.

Black, Allen. Class notes, The Gospel of Mark. Memphis, TN: Harding University Graduate School of Religion, Spring 1995.

Brewer, G. C. *Contending for the Faith.* Nashville, TN: Gospel Advocate Company, 1955.

Broadus, John A. *On the Preparation and Delivery of Sermons*. New and revised edited by Jesse Burton Weatherspoon. New York: Harper & Row, 1944.

Campbell, Alexander. *The Christian System*. Cincinnati, OH: Standard Publishing, n.d.

Carson, D. A., Douglas J. Moo, and Leon Morris. *An Introduction to the New Testament*. Grand Rapids, MI: Zondervan, 1992.

Casey, Maurice. "Culture and Historicity: The Plucking of the Grain (Mark 2:23–28)." *New Testament Studies* 34 (1988): 1–23.

Chadwick, G. A. *The Gospel According to St. Mark*. The Expositor's Bible. Edited by W. Robertson Nicoll. London: Hodder and Stoughton, 1893.

Clark, Gordon H. *Logic*. Jefferson, MD: The Trinity Foundation, 1985, 1988.

Coffman, James Burton. *Commentary on Mark*. Austin, TX: Firm Foundation Publishing, 1975.

Cole, R. A. *The Gospel According to St. Mark*. The Tyndale New Testament Commentaries. Grand Rapids, MI: Eerdmans, 1961.

Collier, Gary D. "An Assessment of the Hermeneutical Impasse in Churches of Christ." Part 2. *Christian Scholars Conference*, 1988.

Cranfield, C. E. B. *The Gospel According to St. Mark*. The Cambridge Greek New Testament Commentary. Cambridge: Cambridge University Press, 1972.

Donahue, R. "Mark." *Harper's Bible Commentary*. Gen. ed. James L. Mays. San Francisco: Harper, 1988.

Dorris, C. E. W. *A Commentary on the Gospel by Mark*. Nashville, TN: Gospel Advocate Company, 1950.

Dowling, Enos, R. C. Foster, Frank H. Marshall, and Orrin Root. *Mark*. Standard Bible Commentary. Cincinnati, OH: Standard Publishing, 1968.

Dunn, James D. "Mark 2.1–3.6: A Bridge Between Jesus and Paul on the Question of the Law." *New Testament Studies* 30 (1984): 395–415.

Fearnside, W. Ward, and William B. Holther. *Fallacy: The Counterfeit of Argument*. Englewood Cliffs, NJ: Prentice Hall, 1959.

Fitzmyer, Joseph A., and Raymond E. Brown, eds. *The Jerome Biblical Commentary*. Volume 2: The New Testament and Topical Articles. Englewood Cliffs, NJ. Prentice Hall, 1968.

Greek New Testament. New York: United Bible Societies, 3rd edition.

Green, Joel B., Scot McKnight, and I. Howard Marshall, eds. *Dictionary of Jesus and the Gospels*. Downers Grove, IL: InterVarsity Press, 1992. s.v. "Mark, Gospel of," by R. A. Guelich. s.v. "Abiathar," by M. R. Mulholland. s.v. "Law," by D. J. Moo. s.v. "Son of Man," by I. H. Marshall.

Gruenler, Royce Gordon. "Mark." *Evangelical Commentary on the Bible*. Edited by Walter A. Elwell. Grand Rapids, MI: Baker Books, 1989.

Hendriksen, William. *New Testament Commentary—Exposition of the Gospel According to Mark*. Grand Rapids, MI: Baker Books, 1975.

Henry, Matthew. *A Commentary on the Holy Bible*. Volume 5. London: Marshall Brothers, n.d.

Hicks, John Mark. "The Sabbath Controversy in Matthew: An Exegesis of Matthew 12:1–14." *Restoration Quarterly* 27 (1984): 79–91.

Hultgren, Arland J. "The Formation of the Sabbath Pericope in Mark 2:23–28." *Journal of Biblical Literature* 91 (1972): 38–43.

Hurley, Patrick J. *A Concise Introduction to Logic.* Belmont, CA: Wadsworth Publishing, 1982.

Lane, William L. *The Gospel According to Mark.* The New International Commentary on the New Testament. Grand Rapids, MI: Eerdmans, 1974.

McGarvey, J. W., and Philip Y. Pendleton, *The Fourfold Gospel.* Cincinnati, OH: Standard Publishing, n.d.

McMillan, Earle. *The Gospel According to Mark.* Austin, TX: Sweet Publishing, 1973.

Metzger, Bruce M. *A Textual Commentary on the Greek New Testament.* New York: United Bible Societies, 1971.

Maule, C. F. D. *Idiom Book of New Testament Greek.* 2nd ed. New York: Cambridge University Press, 1953, 1959.

Osterhaven, M. E. "Sinlessness of Christ." *Evangelical Dictionary of Theology.* Edited by Walter A. Elwell. Grand Rapids, MI: Baker Books, 1984, 1990.

Schweizer, Eduard. *The Good News According to Mark.* Translated by Donald H. Madvig. Atlanta: John Knox Press, 1970.

Sigal, Philip. *Judaism: The Evolution of a Faith.* Grand Rapids, MI: Eerdmans, 1988.

Wessel, Walter W. "Mark." Edited by Frank E. Gaebelein. *The Expositor's Bible Commentary.* Volume 8. Grand Rapids, MI: Zondervan, 1984.

Jesus: "He Went About Doing Good"

BILL AND LAURA S. BAGENTS

We love Peter's famous description of Jesus to Cornelius and his family.

> *God anointed Jesus of Nazareth with the Holy Spirit and with power. He went about doing good and healing all who were oppressed by the devil, for God was with him. (Acts 10:38)*

We love Luke's attention to the actions of Jesus. "In the first book, O Theophilus, I have dealt with all that Jesus began to do and teach" (Acts 1:1). We love the way Scripture urges every disciple to continue the "doing" that Jesus began. "Be steadfast, immovable, always abounding in the work of the Lord" (1 Cor 15:58). "Show yourself in all respects to be a model of good works" (Titus 2:7). Jesus "gave Himself for us to redeem us from all lawlessness and to purify for himself his own possession who are zealous for good works" (Titus 2:14). Faithful leaders remind every

Christian "to be ready for every good work" (Titus 3:1). "Those who have believed in God" are solemnly charged "to be careful to devote themselves to good works" (Titus 3:8). Paul urged Titus to "let our people learn to devote themselves to good works" (Titus 3:14). We dare not forget Colossians 3:17 and 23–24.

> *And whatever you do, in word or deed, do everything in the name of the Lord Jesus, giving thanks to God the Father through him .... Whatever you do, work heartily, as for the Lord and not for men, knowing that from the Lord you will receive the inheritance as your reward. You are serving the Lord Christ.*

As those who are committed to "do all in the name of the Lord," we're wise to look to the gospels—and beyond—and note the actions of Jesus as He lived in the flesh. If we do—as much as possible—as He did, we'll be poised to show Him the highest honor. And we'll be following the greatest of examples.

BEFORE HIS PUBLIC MINISTRY

Even before His public ministry began, Jesus set a powerful example of godly actions. Though He was God and was with God (John 1:1), He "did not count equality with God a thing to be grasped, but he emptied himself, by taking on the form of a servant, being born in the likeness of men" (Phil 2:5ff). What humility, what sacrifice, and what love!

We know amazingly little of the childhood of Jesus, but

what we know is impressive. At age twelve at the temple in Jerusalem, "All who heard him were amazed at his understanding and his answers" (Luke 2:47). Understanding and answers speak of biblical knowledge and spiritual awareness; they turn our thoughts to Psalms 1 and 119. As His parents found Him after a three-day search, His explanation was, "Why were you looking for me? Did you not know that I must be in my Father's house?" (Luke 2:49).

We see the words of Luke 2:51 as summarizing His childhood both before and after the temple visit: "And he went down with them and came to Nazareth and was subject to them." Jesus showed lifelong respect for His mother (John 2:1–11, 19:25–27). At the same time, we love Jesus's steadfast refusal to put His physical family before God (Matt 12:47–50). We love the breadth and balance of Luke 2:52, "And Jesus increased in wisdom and in stature and in favor with God and man."

Shortly before His public work began, Jesus was baptized in the Jordan by John (Matt 3:13–17, Mark 1:1–11). Why would the sinless Son of God be baptized? "Let it be so for this is fitting to fulfill all righteousness" (Matt 3:15). He set a pattern of submission and obedience for us to follow.

Immediately after His baptism, "Jesus was led up by the Spirit into the wilderness to be tempted by the devil" (Matt 4:1–11). Both weakened (physically) and strengthened (spiritually) by forty days of fasting, He defeated Satan at a level that made the devil withdraw "until an opportune time" (Luke 4:13).

Even as His public ministry began, Luke subtly reminds us of another of Jesus's regular practices: "And he came to

Nazareth, where he had been brought up. And as was his custom, he went to the synagogue on the Sabbath day, and he stood up to read" (Luke 4:13). He didn't just attend; He was an active, contributing worshipper (Heb 10:24).

To summarize, even before His public ministry started, Jesus

1. Demonstrated humility, sacrifice, and love at the highest possible levels.
2. Prepared Himself for life and service through the ongoing learning of God's will.
3. Honored and obeyed His parents.
4. Grew in a well-ordered, balanced, God-honoring way.
5. Embraced a life of righteousness.
6. Followed the leading of God's Spirit.
7. Faced and defeated temptation through reliance on God's word.
8. Regularly participated in corporate worship.

DURING HIS PUBLIC MINISTRY

Matthew 4:17 offers a key way to understand Jesus's public ministry: "From that time Jesus began to preach, saying, 'Repent for the kingdom of heaven is at hand.'" Luke 4:31–32 and Matthew 4:23 remind us not to make too much distinction between preaching and teaching. He proclaimed and explained; He warned and informed. In word and deed, He encouraged both repentance and godly living. Jesus called others to heightened levels of spiritual service (Matt 4:18–22, 10:1–32).

We do not possess the miraculous power of Jesus, but we love His example of helping and healing "every disease and every affliction" and welcoming people to bring "all the sick" to Him (Matt 4:23–25). We love the fact that He rejected both favoritism and financial exploitation. We love the way He praised the faith of those who trusted God (Matt 8:10–12, 9:22 & 29, 15:28). We love His practice of compassion (Matt 9:36). And we love His wisdom in limiting His actions when the people chose not to believe even in the face of mighty acts (Matt 13:53–58).

Jesus definitively corrected misunderstanding and misapplication of Scripture: "You have heard that it was said to those of old" (Matt 5:21, 27, 31, 33, 38, 43). He courageously opposed religious leaders who added to God's law and "shut the kingdom of God in people's faces (Matt 23:13). How stunning! The scribes and Pharisees "shut the kingdom" while Jesus described Himself as "the door of the sheep" (John 10:7 & 9).

Jesus did not allow people to follow Him without first counting the cost of discipleship (Matt 8:18–22, 10:18–23; John 6:22–27). He welcomed followers—not on their terms —but on God's (Luke 9:23–26). He never tried to buy—or rent—followers. From the beginning of His work, He rejected shallow sensationalism (Matt 4:5–7). Though it must have broken His heart, He let people walk away when they chose to do so (Mark 10:17–22, John 6:66).

Jesus dealt effectively with critics. He did not let them control either His attitude or His actions (Matt 9:1–7). He didn't let potential criticism keep Him from calling Matthew, eating in Matthew's house, or preaching the good news to Matthew's fellow tax collectors (Matt 9:8–13). He even ate with a Pharisee (Luke 7:36–50). When appropriate, He answered criticism with Scripture and logic (Matt 12:22–37, 15:1–9), but He refused to perform signs on demand (Matt 12:38–45). And on other occasions, "He made no answer" (Luke 23:9, Matt 21:23–27). As needed, he raised the level of the question posed to Him (Matt 22:16–22). He quoted and explained Old Testament teaching, affirming creation (Matt 19:1–9) and the story of Jonah and the fish (Matt 12:38–41, 16:4). When proper, He bluntly exposed errant doctrine (Matt 22:23–33). He adapted His teaching—specifically through parables—so that true seekers could find, and scoffers would be left willfully blind (Matt 13:10–13).

Jesus practiced welcoming openness and transparency in ministry (John 18:19–21). He endured insult and indignity with grace (Luke 4:16–25, 1 Pet 2:21–24). He both urged and practiced interpersonal forgiveness (Matt 6:14–15 & 18:21–35, Luke 23:34 & 43). He affirmed God's forgiveness at a level far beyond the religious teachers of His day (John 8:1–11). He both taught and demonstrated that greatness in God's kingdom comes through service (Luke 9:46–48, John 13:1–11).

Jesus refused to be limited by social conventions when they would have limited His ability to do good and to teach the gospel:

- He healed a centurion's servant at a time when Roman soldiers occupied His homeland (Matt 8:1–13).
- He healed on the Sabbath (Mark 3:1–6).

- He touched a leper as part of the man's healing (Luke 5:13).
- He rejected unjust criticism of His disciples because it was based on human tradition (Mark 7:1–13).
- He valued the gifts of even the poorest people (Mark 12:41–44).
- He allowed a sinful woman to anoint Him (Luke 7:36–50). He treated her like she mattered.
- He allowed people who had been possessed by demons to follow Him and to give glory to God (Luke 8:1–3 & 38–39).
- He told the parable we know as "The Good Samaritan" (Luke 10:30–37).
- He talked with and accepted help from a Samaritan woman (John 4:1–42).
- He praised the faith of a thankful Samaritan (Luke 17:12–19).
- He called a rich chief tax collector "a son of Abraham" as He announced that salvation had come to Zacchaeus's house (Luke 19:1–10).
- He drove profiteering money changers out of the temple (Luke 19:45–48).
- He approved paying taxes to Caesar (Luke 29:20–26).
- He gave sinful people a second chance (John 8:1–12, 21:15–20).
- He washed feet like a slave or servant (John 13:1–20).

To summarize, during His public ministry, Jesus

1. Treated God's word as authoritative and worthy of respect.
2. Opposed the teaching of religious error.
3. Called people to repentance and righteousness.
4. Respected people's right to accept or reject His message.
5. Continually helped people with the goal of their salvation from sin.
6. Refused to let critics define or limit Him.
7. Urged and practiced amazing forgiveness.
8. Overcame social conventions that could have limited His work.

AFTER HIS DEATH AND RESURRECTION

Just as the actions of the Son of God began before His birth as a human, they continue after His ascension from earth. We appreciate His encouraging words to the disciples who awaited the birth of the kingdom at Pentecost (Acts 2:1–9). At the time of God's choosing, the promise of the kingdom would be fulfilled. His disciples would bear witness of Him "even to the end of the earth" (Acts 1:7). God's words are in themselves actions; what God promises is as good as done (Heb 11:13, 2 Pet 3:1–9).

We both love and shudder at the scene recorded in Acts 7:54–60. In Stephen's final moments, he "saw the glory of God and Jesus standing at the right hand of God." It's repeated for emphasis. Whether standing out of concern, out of respect, in support, or some combination, we love what Jesus did for His courageous servant.

Jesus also appears in Acts 9, getting the attention and changing the world of Saul the persecutor. From his new understanding of blindness—both physical and spiritual—Saul was ready to be told "what you are to do" (Acts 9:6). Jesus prepared Saul, informed him of his future work, prepared Ananias to teach Saul, and washed Saul's sins away as he was baptized for remission of sin (Acts 2:38, 22:16). And we find ourselves commissioned for the same soul-saving purpose (Matt 28:18–20, Mark 16:15–16).

Acts 23:11 records another of Jesus's acts of love, comfort, and support. During one of Paul's darkest hours, he heard directly from the Lord: "Take courage, for as you have testified to the facts about me in Jerusalem, so you must testify also in Rome." In so few words, Paul learned so much. "I won't die immediately—God will deliver. By God's grace, I'll realize my longtime dream of preaching in Rome (Rom 1:8–13). My work for God is not yet done!"

We dare not forget the words of love, hope, warning, comfort, judgment, and correction delivered from Jesus to the seven churches of Asia (Rev 2–3). Jesus knew the trials and pressures faced by each church. He also knew both their actions and their motives. Their souls and service mattered to Him. Even as He graciously offered an additional measure of patience, He made clear that they were "on the clock." If they didn't act, He would. Jesus knows us just as well and holds us just as accountable.

We also delight in remembering that "Christ Jesus is He who died—more than that, who was raised—who is at the right hand of God, who indeed is interceding for us"

(Rom 8:34). "He always lives to make intercession for [us]" (Heb 7:25). And He said of Himself, "I go to prepare a place for you. And if I go and prepare a place for you, I will come again and will take you to myself, that where I am you may be also" (John 14:2b-3). As He prepares for us, we're both wise and blessed to prepare for His return.

To summarize, Jesus continues to

1. Encourage His disciples through Scripture, through providence, and through the faithful support of other Christians.
2. Evangelize through those who follow in His steps (Luke 19:10).
3. Comfort those who struggle (2 Cor 1:3–4).
4. Expect His bride, His church, to love, to serve, and to be "holy and without blemish" (Eph 5:27).

RESPONSES TO JESUS'S ACTIONS

Though Jesus did nothing but good and always honored God's will (John 8:27, 1 Pet 2:21–22), His actions met with wildly diverse reactions. During periods of His ministry, both individuals and multitudes followed Him enthusiastically (Matt 4:20 & 25). Ultimately, droves of disciples left Him (John 6:66). Even His closest followers fled (Matt 26:56). The crowd that welcomed Him to Jerusalem as their king (Matt 21:1–11), only a short time later shouted, "Away with him, away with him, crucify him" (John 19:15).

During a major period of His ministry, many people "heard him gladly" (Mark 12:37) and were "astonished at his teaching" (Matt 7:28). On multiple occasions, they marveled at His miracles (Matt 8:27, 9:8 & 33, 15:30–31). They even tried to make Him king by force (John 6:15). How ironic that John 6 also records their fickleness when they encountered more challenging truth (John 6:52 & 60).

Even during the periods of great popularity with the people, there were exceptions: "And behold, the whole city came out to meet Jesus, and when they saw him, they begged him to leave their region" (Matt 8:37). At one point, a village of Samaritans "did not receive him, because his face was set toward Jerusalem" (Luke 9:53).

During the bulk of His public ministry, the religious leaders opposed Jesus. "Some of the scribes said to themselves, 'This man is blaspheming'" (Matt 9:3). The Pharisees accused Him of working for and through Satan (Matt 9:34, 12:24). They questioned both His identity (Matt 11:1–3, 13:52–58) and His authority (Matt 21:23–27). On many occasions, they tried to trap Jesus with questions and hypothetical situations (Matt 15:1–2, 17:24, 19:1 & 7, 20:20–23, 22:15–18 & 23–32 & 34–36). They demanded signs from Him (Matt 12:38, 16:1). Ultimately, they plotted to kill Him and put both money and false witnesses behind their plot (Matt 11:14, 21:45–48, 26:14–15).

The responses of Jesus's disciples to His words and deeds were sometimes stellar. Think of Peter's confession (Matt 16:16) and the to-the-death loyalty of Thomas (John 11:16). On other occasions, the disciples stunningly disappointed Him. After his beautiful confession, Peter rebuked the Lord (Matt 16:22). Some of the disciples were indignant when Jesus wastefully—in their eyes—allowed a woman to anoint Him with "very costly fragrant oil" (Matt 26:6–13). Peter, at first, refused to let Jesus wash his feet (John 13:8).

Peter bluntly denied a prophecy of Jesus (Matt 26:31–35). In the hour of His greatest need for prayer and support, the three disciples who were closest to Him fell asleep—three times (Matt 26:36–46). Even more amazingly, some of the disciples—and not just Thomas—had doubts even after seeing the resurrected Christ: "And when they saw him, they worshiped him, but some doubted" (Matt 28:17, John 20:27–30).

One question remains: What did God the Father do in response to Jesus's perfect life? He validated, vindicated, raised, and glorified His Son forever. Jesus knew this: "All authority in heaven and on earth has been given to me" (Matt 28:18). Peter made it the center of his Pentecost sermon: "Let all the house of Israel therefore know for certain that God has made him both Lord and Christ, this Jesus whom you crucified" (Acts 2:36). Paul states it beautifully:

> *Therefore God has exalted him and bestowed on him the name that is above every name, so that at the name of Jesus every knee should bow, in heaven and on earth, and every tongue confess that Jesus Christ is Lord, to the glory of God the Father (Phil 2:9–11)*

And John the apostle summarizes by lauding Jesus as "the faithful witness, the firstborn of the dead, and the ruler of kings on earth" (Rev 1:5).

CONCLUSION

What an honor to be able, empowered, commanded, and blessed to walk in our Lord's steps. To be like Him, we must do as He did. "A disciple is not above his teacher, but everyone when he is fully trained will be like his teacher" (Luke 6:40). "A disciple is not above his teacher, nor a servant above his master. It is enough for the disciple to be like his teacher and the servant like his master" (Matt 10:24–25).

What a benefit and protection to know that even as we imitate our Lord, our actions will be met with mixed reviews. As in Acts 2, some will be cut to the heart and immediately seek salvation while others will mock. Though we can never be sure of human reactions, we can always be sure of God's perfectly stable goodness. It is wondrous, blessed, and more than enough to be like Jesus by doing as Jesus did.

The Syrophoenician Woman

MARK 7:24-30

THOMAS TIDWELL

❧

Jesus cares for and loves deeply for all men and women, and He desires that all, regardless of socioeconomic background, race, or the sin they are engaged in, to be saved (1 Tim 2:4).

One of the most fascinating studies that we should consider is the study of Jesus's interaction with women.

Consider Jesus's interaction with Mary, His mother. He loved her, no doubt because she was his mother. We can only imagine how Jesus struggled with his mother when she asked him to do something that did not follow His will. In John 2 Jesus seemingly rebukes his mother by saying, "*Woman, what does your concern have to do with me? My hour has not yet come,*" when the host ran out of wine at a wedding. It says much about Mary that she came to Jesus and knew he could solve her problem.

In Luke 8:19–21, we see the record of Jesus's mother and brothers coming to him, perhaps to deal with a family matter. When Jesus was told this, he stated, "*My mother and*

My brothers are those who hear the word of God and do it." In this phrase Jesus clearly shows that his relatives are those who do the Father's will; hence, all who follow the Father are his relatives.

We consider Jesus's interaction with Mary and Martha, sisters of Lazarus. In Luke 10:38–42 Martha welcomed Jesus into her home, in order to feed him and allow him to rest. Mary stayed at Jesus's feet to listen to Jesus teach; Mary was perturbed because she was working to feed those who were there. (Most women I have met are always very concerned when company comes over and they are "entertaining." They want everything to be just right—and I am thankful for the work and effort they put forth in doing this!).

In Jesus's interaction with the woman taken in adultery in John 8, we see that Jesus saw through the trap that the scribes and Pharisees laid by bringing a woman taken in adultery, *"in the very act."* Jesus saw through their ruse and stated *"He who is without sin among you, let him throw a stone at her first."* (John 8:7). He did not condone her sin, and did not condemn her because the accusers had walked away. But he gives her hope—*"go and sin no more."*

For the remainder of this study let us look at the story of Jesus dealing with a Gentile woman whose daughter had an unclean spirit.

> *And from there he arose and went away to the region of Tyre and Sidon. And he entered a house and did not want anyone to know, yet he could not be hidden. But immediately a woman whose little daughter had an unclean spirit heard of him and came and fell down at his feet. Now the woman was a Gentile, a*

Syrophoenician by birth. And she begged him to cast the demon out of her daughter. And he said to her, "Let the children be fed first, for it is not right to take the children's bread and throw it to the dogs." But she answered him, "Yes, Lord; yet even the dogs under the table eat the children's crumbs." And he said to her, "For this statement you may go your way; the demon has left your daughter." And she went home and found the child lying in bed and the demon gone (Mark 7:24-30).

As we look at this event, notice these facts:

Jesus needed to get away and rest, hence, He went to the region of Tyre and Sidon, yet He could not be hidden. We all need our rest—especially the women who work an outside job and then go home to feed and take care of their families.

When the woman who had a demon-possessed child found that Jesus was there, she did what any loving mother would do for her children. She fell at the feet of Jesus and asked that He heal her daughter. Mothers worry about their children. They worry about their future, they worry when they are sick, and worry when trouble comes to them. They never stop being concerned about their children, even when the children are grown and have their own families. Moms will move heaven and earth to help their children. (I know, as my mom would do the same for me, and my wife does the same for our children.)

This woman was bold in that she was a Gentile, and she dared make her request to Jesus, a Jewish rabbi. The prejudices between Jews and Gentiles were clearly known, stemming from God's word in the Old Testament that the Israelites should not interact with the people of the world.

(Abraham would not allow his son Isaac to intermarry with the people of the land as recorded in Genesis 24:3 and Genesis 24:37. Isaac forbade Jacob to take a wife from the daughters of Canaan in Genesis 28:1. Mosaic law was specific in Deuteronomy 7:1–4, and Joshua warned against this in Joshua 23:12. Other passages to examine are Judges 3:6; Judges 14:3; 1 Kings 3:1–11, 16:31; 2 Chronicles 8:11; and Ezra 9:12; 10:14; 10:44.

When she asked that Jesus deal with the demon in her daughter, Jesus responded, *"Let the children be fed first, for it is not right to take the children's bread and throw it to the dogs."* Perhaps Jesus was testing her, for she was a Gentile and a woman. The Jews considered the Gentiles as dogs, and Jesus wanted to see her response.

> *But she answered him, "Yes, Lord; yet even the dogs under the table eat the children's crumbs." And he said to her, "For this statement you may go your way; the demon has left your daughter." And she went home and found the child lying in bed and the demon gone.*

Look at the statement of faith this woman uttered. She said, "I don't want the children to miss out on anything they need—all I am asking for is the crumbs that fall from the table." Dogs often eat crumbs around a table when the family is eating—and she said to Jesus, that she said she just wanted crumbs for her child. Jesus understood and healed her daughter.

Mothers will do anything for their children, even if it means embarrassing themselves. A mother's love motivated her to ask for help for her child, and she would be satisfied with what Jesus would do, however insignificant.

Mothers will die for their children if necessary. Where do men and women learn that kind of love? God the Father, Jesus the Son, and the Holy Spirit planned the salvation of mankind through the death of Jesus. They exemplified love when Jesus willingly died for us—His children. Mothers have the heart of God in that respect—from the time of conception till birth, and then afterward.

In the church today, women often show more faith in God than men. They see the need for God in their lives, and some of the best Christians are women who are known for the things they do behind the scenes for the church. They meet and encourage one another. They are willing to do whatever is necessary to aid the sick and often do much more visiting than men. We could not live without women fixing food for fellowship meals.

So many today in our world believe women should be preachers, elders, deacons, and leaders of all kinds of programs in opposition to 1 Timothy 2:9–15. Why?

Many men today are not stepping up to the positions of responsibilities they need to because they consider the church to be too "feminized." Many men will not do things they see that need to be done because they are too busy with jobs, recreation, and other things.

Jesus honored the faith of men and women time and again. God knows that both are necessary for the home and for the church. Therefore, it is imperative that husbands should love their wives as Christ loved (and still loves) the church—(Eph 5:25).

Ladies who are serving behind the scenes –
THANK YOU.

May God give us more male and female workers who have the faith in Jesus to do the work that needs to be done.

What great things will we ask of our Lord; and what great things will we all do for our Lord?

Disruptive Kindness

TRAVIS HARMON

FIRST DISCLAIMER

Kindness. I need this. I really need this lesson. I need this so badly; it is obvious. I was standing in my driveway one day talking to two preacher friends. One of them asked, "What are you preaching tomorrow?" It's a question people often ask a preacher on a Saturday. I gave them the overview of my planned lesson on kindness, and we talked for a while. One of the two guys looked at me and cocked his head sideways and said, "You, are going to talk about that?" He really put the emphasis on the "You" and the "that." "YOU, are going to talk about THAT?" I had to sheepishly tell him, that is exactly why "I" needed to talk about "that." I think I had to emphasize every word in that sentence. I knew I needed this one. I need it badly. I NEED IT BADLY.

SECOND DISCLAIMER

I am talking about kindness, so I need to clarify what I'm not talking about here. I am not talking about pacifism and saying you cannot defend loved ones. I'm not talking about allowing yourself to be inappropriately abused. I am not saying you cannot vote or interact with politics. I am not talking about ignoring justice. I am not talking about being a passive boss or a permissive parent who never disciplines, and I am not talking about being a pushover. I am talking about Biblical levels of kindness.

MALICIOUS COMPLIANCE

I love terms like malicious compliance. It is an oxymoron, of a sort. It is like "passive-aggressive." Well, it's exactly like passive-aggressive. It is passive-aggressive. Wikipedia says,

> Malicious compliance (also known as malicious obedience) is the behavior of strictly following the orders of a superior despite knowing that compliance with the orders will have an unintended or negative result.

When you go along with the order or request knowing it will have a disastrous effect, you do it anyway intentionally to cause the disastrous effect.

Malicious compliance happens all the time in situations where there is a quota, some projection, or production number that must be met. It happens especially when there's poor morale or a lack of trust between workers and supervisors. It happens all the time with homeowners' associations. People observe the letter of the law but they're violating the intent of the law. Like the guy who got a letter from the HOA that said his mailbox had to be red so he slopped paint all over the wall and covered the mailbox. His mailbox is now red. He violated the spirit of the law but complied with the rule.

Before I left Arkansas on my last week as a police officer, I got in a high-speed chase with a vehicle that turned out to be driven by a 90-year-old. He had rammed the office of the apartment complex he lived in with his Cadillac at 2 am over some dispute and then sped off. He was the only other car on the road when he passed me going 95 mph. I turned around with my lights on, and when he saw me, he eventually slowed down to 45 mph, but he did not stop. I followed him for fifteen miles until Jonesboro PD spiked his tires. Then he drove on until he had nothing but rims. He stopped only when he did not have the traction to make it up an overpass. He was spunky, and he always reminded me of malicious compliance.

Once, years before he had wanted to build on to his house, and the city would not approve his addition, so he built a massive brick arch over his driveway. It was in code, but it was a huge eyesore! There was no rule against it, and therefore he did it just out of spite. He then had "Fort Defiance" in huge letters put on the arch. True malicious compliance.

Malicious compliance is a common motif in movies, books, and stories when people need to get their comeuppance. Like the story of the staff at a wing restaurant that served a pound of wings for a low price every Thursday night. They didn't weigh the wings but guessed at it and thought eight was about a pound, so they just sold eight wings as a pound. One night a guest said, "We all ordered the pound of wings, and everyone's plate has exactly eight wings! That is a huge coincidence, isn't it? Weigh these wings to make sure I'm getting what I paid for!" The server weighed the wings and, sure enough, it was not a pound. The server brought them back and said like a smiling serpent, "Here are your wings, sir. You were right! Here is your 1.03 pound of wings! We had to take two of them off to get it down to a pound."

Malicious compliance. There is a verse that always reminds me of that. "Therefore if thine enemy hunger, feed him; if he thirsts, give him drink: for in so doing thou shalt heap coals of fire on his head" (Rom 12:20). It is a quote from Proverbs 25:22 "In doing this, you will heap burning coals on his head, and the LORD will reward you."

I think I know a lot of people who follow that verse with malicious compliance. What they want is to make the other person mad. Super mad! "Remember to be nice because it will make the other person SO MAD!" I am sure that is not the point of the verse. Look at Romans 12:1–2 and read all of Romans 12:14–21. It is certainly not intended to be passive-aggressive, and it is not to be followed with malicious compliance. It is about audacious, jaw-dropping, seemingly irresponsible kindness.

DISRUPTIVE KINDNESS

Christianity teaches us to be irresponsibly kind by human standards. The world tells us the way to peace is a bigger stick, a bigger gun, a nuclear weapon. Achieve peace via a force greater than your rival. Christianity says the way to peace is through kindness: overt, absurd, audacious, impractical kindness, a stop-them-in-their-tracks, expose-their-evil, leave-them-speechless level of kindness.

Jesus taught this level of kindness, this absurd, audacious, stunning, seemingly irresponsible kindness. He and His followers taught this level of kindness. To humans, it is near reprehensible levels of forgiveness. To us, it is appalling levels of mercy and imprudent levels of generosity. This is a Romans 12:17–21 kindness.

Jesus taught this in Matthew 5:38–48.

> You have heard that it was said, 'Eye for eye, and tooth for tooth.' But I tell you, do not resist an evil person. If anyone slaps you on the right cheek, turn to them the other cheek also. And if anyone wants to sue you and take your shirt, hand over your coat as well. If anyone forces you to go one mile, go with them two miles. Give to the one who asks you, and do not turn away from the one who wants to borrow from you. You have heard that it was said, "Love your neighbor and hate your enemy." But I tell you, love your enemies and pray for those who persecute you, that you may be children of your Father in heaven. He causes his sun to rise on the evil and the good and sends rain on the righteous and the unrighteous. If you love those who love you, what reward will you get?

Are not even the tax collectors doing that? And if you greet only your own people, what are you doing more than others? Do not even pagans do that? Be perfect, therefore, as your heavenly Father is perfect.

Don't revile. Don't return evil for evil. Love those who persecute you, and pray for those who slander you. Don't follow Matthew 5 with malicious compliance but with stunning, incomprehensible, irresponsible kindness. He set that example too. Jesus's life displayed disruptive kindness. He did not just teach it, He lived it.

In John 13:1–17 He washes the disciples' feet, a powerful lesson on servanthood and humility. The leader loves and serves. It is a great lesson. It is shocking to realize how John is intentionally reminding the reader Judas is there. He has not left yet, and Peter is there also. The two that will most powerfully betray Him. He takes those feet in His hands and with gentleness and kindness washes their feet. That is a powerful image of incomprehensible levels of assertive forgiveness and kindness.

In Luke 22:47–52, He is betrayed with a kiss by this man with bloody hands and clean feet. Judas's hands are covered by the blood of the man whose hands had just washed his feet.

In verse 51, He heals the ear of one of those who came to arrest and murder him. This is a seemingly irresponsible act of kindness that is going to result in His death. Then Peter disowns Him in verse 54, and the guards mock Him in verse 63.

In Luke 23:35, He asks for those who were crucifying Him to be forgiven. That is stunning. It is why He came: to

DISRUPTIVE KINDNESS

offer audacious forgiveness and show incomprehensible kindness.

In Luke 23:43, He forgives the criminal on the cross. Overt, absurd, audacious kindness. Stop-them-in-their tracks kindness. It feels like irresponsible levels of kindness. These actions display insane levels of forgiveness, disturbing levels of mercy, imprudent levels of generosity, and just disruptive levels of kindness.

In *Les Miserables*, Jean Valjean only knows how to be a criminal after spending 19 years in prison for stealing a loaf of bread to feed his family. Yet fate casts him into the life of a bishop one night who shows him true and genuine kindness. The bishop gives him dinner and a room for the night in a time when that was unheard of. Valjean is shaken by the kindness. Still, he steals the bishop's silverware and flees. He's captured by the police and brought back to the bishop who, in an unfathomable act of irresponsible and disruptive kindness, pretends he had given the silverware to Valjean. To prove it, he gives Jean his last silver candlesticks to convince the police that nothing was stolen. This act changes Valjean forever. Disruptive kindness.

Mike Birbiglia. Mike is a well-liked comedian. He has done a lot of comedy specials and is on the radio often. He is a fantastic storyteller, the kind that a listener feels compelled to listen to. He just makes his audience chuckle the entire time, even when he is telling a story that should not really be funny.

He does this bit about how he was hit by a drunk driver. The way he describes the entire event is sad but makes the listener chuckle the entire time. At one emotional point in the story, he tells how he realized he almost died. The guy t-boned him, and he was really shaken. It was a hit-and-run, but the guy did not get far because he hit a tree a few yards down the road. Mike calls it a hit-and-run-and-hit. Mike's friend took him to the hospital, and he had to wait an hour because the doctor was treating the drunk driver first. A few days later, the insurance company calls and says he owes $12,000 to pay for the drunk guy's car.

Mike was wrongly listed as being at fault on the accident report. He says the accident report is like homework for cops, and that Officer Timpson was apparently not so good with homework. The report was just a mess. Everything was confusing and even sounded like it had Mike crashing into himself. He called the police station and talked to the officer's supervisor. He tried to argue his case, but the lieutenant said, "You made a bad turn so do the right thing and pay for the guy's car." He tried to further discuss it, and over and over, the officer said, "You made a mistake. Do the right thing and pay for the guy's car." He became obsessed over the next few weeks. He printed off laws and called everyone he could. He started making a case like he was in a crime drama. He said, "I am in the right! This is about justice!" He became so obsessed it was all he talked about and so people stopped talking to him.

He was at dinner with his girlfriend one night, and all he could talk about was the case. She looked at him and said, "You are right, but you are only hurting yourself." He said she only had to say it once. He paid for the guy's car. He said he has given up on the idea of being right.

Yeah, he paid $12,000 for the other guy's car. I heard that story years ago, and it has always bothered me! How can our system get it so wrong?! It happens. It happens all the time in little ways and big ways. Someone does wrong and someone is willing to go to prison to get even because he/she was right! I want the other guy to pay! I want justice! I want the officer reprimanded! I want it set right, and I want Mike to fight this thing. It disturbs me that he just paid for the guy's car! Honestly, it has disrupted my life because every time I think of the story, it messes with me.

Maybe Jesus wants him to do just what Mike did ... Matthew 5:38-40.

> You have heard that it was said, "Eye for eye, and tooth for tooth." But I tell you, do not resist an evil person. If anyone slaps you on the right cheek, turn to them the other cheek also. And if anyone wants to sue you and take your shirt, hand over your coat as well.

THAT is disruptive kindness.
Colossians 3:12-13

> Put on then, as God's chosen ones, holy and beloved, compassionate hearts, kindness, humility, meekness, and patience, bearing with one another and, if one has a complaint against another, forgiving each other; as the Lord has forgiven you, so you also must forgive.

As the Lord has forgiven you. Wow.
It is a Fruit of the Spirit. Galatians 5:22-23

But the fruit of the Spirit is love, joy, peace, forbearance, kindness, goodness, faithfulness, gentleness and self-control.

Galatians 6:10

So then, as we have opportunity, let us do good to everyone, and especially to those who are of the household of faith.

As we have an opportunity? Every opportunity? Ephesians 4:29–32.

Let no corrupt communication proceed out of your mouth, but that which is good to the use of edifying, that it may minister grace unto the hearers. And grieve not the holy Spirit of God, whereby ye are sealed unto the day of redemption. Let all bitterness, and wrath, and anger, and clamour, and evil speaking, be put away from you, with all malice: and be ye kind one to another, tenderhearted, forgiving one another, even as God for Christ's sake hath forgiven you.

Kind, tenderhearted, forgiving <u>AS</u> God has forgiven us? Jesus did not call us to fight for our rights. I see so many Christians who will "not be spoken to in this manner!" Christians who "demand my rights!" and those who "want everything that is mine!" Christians, of all the people in the world, should be okay with a little mistreatment and understand how they should respond to it. Be nice to the waitress, even if she is bad. Like, even if she is mean to you on purpose. Be kind to the person in the wrong, especially when you are in the right.

People don't always act on a belief. Someone can believe that smoking will cause bodily harm and light a cigarette right up. Christians don't always act on their beliefs, and they don't always act like Christ. We know we're supposed to be nice. I think we know Jesus teaches us that we're supposed to be outlandishly nice.

How to change the world is not through force or legislation, but through kindness. Audacious, disruptive kindness. Not a bigger gun, but bigger kindness.

If you want peace, be peaceful. If you want kindness, be kind. Change the world, not by force, but through RIGHTEOUS compliance and disruptive kindness.

What if everyone was Christlike? What if everyone did not respond in anger? What if everyone acted like an idyllic Christian? That's how we change the world. That's what we need. You say everyone will not be kind and then the evil will abuse those who are kind? Yep. That's true. That is Christianity. That was Jesus's life in a nutshell.

> I think probably kindness is my number one attribute in a human being. I'll put it before any of the things like courage or bravery or generosity or anything else. —Roald Dahl.

I think he's right. It does take a lot of bravery and courage and generosity to be kind though. If I had to spend a lot of time with one person, I think I would want their number one quality to be kindness. I think that it is also an important quality if we want to spend a lot of time with Christ. I think He likes that in people He spends time with. I know He does.

I can't offer an invitation to come forward and be baptized or repent. The invitation I can extend is to go forth and be kind. Someone who wants to repent should never wait for a second to do that, and we probably shouldn't wait for a second longer to start being kinder. Oh, that we were all changed in the same way by the Father giving us His Light of the World as Valjean with his candlesticks.

THIRD DISCLAIMER

I want to be irresponsibly kind by human standards. Jesus levels of kind. We do not need to be the people who give anyone their comeuppance. I don't want mine. So many people have Fort Defiance on their hearts, but as Christians, we need to have Fort Compliance over our hearts. Not malicious compliance, but disruptively kind.

For Mechelle Thompson, one who is truly disruptively kind.

Here I Am to Do Community Outreach

MELISSA MCFERRIN

W e understand that love means caring, not only in the sense of inner goodwill toward a person, but also in the sense of outward actions on that person's behalf. Ephesians 5:28–30 says,

> So husbands ought also to love their own wives as their own bodies. He who loves his own wife loves himself; for no one ever hated his own flesh, but nourishes and cherishes it, just as Christ also does the church, because we are members of His body (NASB1995).

Those words "nourish" and "cherish" encompass the full range of physical and emotional care which we naturally try to do for ourselves and also to extend to our spouses.

But Christian love reaches beyond ourselves and our families. The command "You shall love your neighbor as yourself" is repeated ten times in the Bible (Lev 19:18; Matt 5:43; 19:19; 22:39; Mark 12:31, 33; Luke 10:27; Rom 13:8–10;

Gal 5:14; Jas 2:8) and alluded to several more. If you're wondering what it means to love your neighbor, apply the golden rule (Matt 7:12). Think about your basic needs: water, food, clothing, shelter, safety, medical care, education, transportation, community, etc. Loving your neighbors, in large part, means providing those things for them. Of course, the deepest need is one they might not know they have, which is the need for God. One of the greatest expressions of love for your neighbors involves sharing the gospel with them.

Loving your neighbors is the basis for community outreach. Here, motivation matters. As Paul exclaimed, "If I give all my possessions to feed the poor, and if I surrender my body to be burned, but do not have love, it profits me nothing" (1 Cor 13:3). If you love your neighbors, you will want to see both their *material* and their *spiritual* needs met. Community outreach, then, includes benevolence, but it is not only benevolence; it includes evangelism, but it is not only evangelism. Community outreach is also more than letting your light shine as you go about your life (Matt 5:16; Phil 2:15).

I define community outreach as *a deliberate attempt to form connections by showing interest and care for the purpose of drawing people to God.*

This should go without saying, but community outreach focuses on the *community*, the unbelievers who live around you. Some members of the church may also be on the receiving end, but they are not the primary audience. Some efforts may serve the entire community, and some may focus on a specific segment. There are many different ways it can be done, so we will examine a few principles and leave the specifics up to you, in your context, in your community.

Principle 1: Actually, we have already talked about this one, but it's so important that it bears repeating. Community outreach flows out of a love for your neighbors and a desire to see them cared for and brought near to God.

Principle 2: Pray about it. Remember that, although your role is vital, your efforts are not ultimately responsible for the endeavor's success or failure. Ask God for blessings, guidance, and whatever else you need. Pray for your audience and their receptivity. Paul wrote to Timothy,

> First of all, then, I urge that entreaties and prayers, petitions and thanksgivings, be made on behalf of all men, for kings and all who are in authority, so that we may lead a tranquil and quiet life in all godliness and dignity. This is good and acceptable in the sight of God our Savior, who desires all men to be saved and to come to the knowledge of the truth (1 Tim 2:1–4).

Pray also for yourself, your boldness, and your work. Consider the example of the Christians who prayed with Peter and John:

> And now, Lord, take note of their [the Jewish leaders'] threats, and grant that Your bond-servants may speak Your word with all confidence, while You extend Your hand to heal, and signs and wonders take place through the name of Your holy servant Jesus (Acts 4:29–30).

They worked, but they entrusted the effectiveness to God.

Principle 3: In general, community outreach works best among the needy. I'm not talking only about the poor, but anyone with a felt need that you can help fulfill. The verses we just read mentioned healing, which was a major method of outreach for the apostles.

- Peter and John healed the lame beggar in Jerusalem (Acts 3:1–10).
- Peter and the disciples healed others in Jerusalem (Acts 5:15–16).
- Philip healed in Samaria (Acts 8:6–8).
- Paul healed the crippled man in Lystra (Acts 14:8–10).
- Paul healed in Ephesus (Acts 19:11–12).
- Paul healed Publius' father and others in Malta (Acts 28:8–9).

Since we don't have the miraculous power of healing, we have to adapt to our capabilities. Maybe you have medical training you can put to use, maybe you can be an encouragement and comfort, maybe you can ease a financial burden, or maybe you can be available for spiritual conversations. Those who are facing medical challenges are acutely aware of their need and, in many cases, their mortality as well.

"Needy" frequently does mean poor, though. People among the lower economic levels are often more receptive to assistance. The Christian leaders in Jerusalem "asked us to remember the poor—the very thing I also was eager to do," Paul wrote (Gal 2:10). Dorcas made clothes for widows (Acts 9:39). Cornelius was praised for giving alms to the poor (Acts 10:1–2). Poverty, terrible as it is, provides a wide-open opportunity for food pantries, community closets, school supply giveaways, and Christmas boxes. All of these show care and are pathways to developing relationships with non-Christians and drawing them in.

There are many other kinds of needs—disaster relief, job placement assistance, help for new immigrants, and the list goes on. Take stock of your community. Where are there holes you can fill? Start there.

Principle 4: You're not any better than they are. It's easy to fall into thinking, "I am doing good things for these people who aren't as _____ as I am." Resist that attitude. Remember, "Such were some of you; but you were washed, but you were sanctified, but you were justified in the name of the Lord Jesus Christ and in the Spirit of our God" (1 Cor 6:11). We are all sinners dependent on the grace of God.

Romans 11 reminds us that we were grafted into God's family, and God will graft in anyone else who comes to faith (Rom 11:17–24). "Do not be arrogant," the passage warns, "Remember that it is not you who supports the root, but the root supports you" (Rom 11:18). As we mentioned when we talked about prayer, we're able to do anything only because of the power of God, only because He has made us His children and charged us to be His hands and feet in the world. Keeping this in mind is important. People can sense what you think of them.

Since we were just speaking about the poor, listen to what James said in James 2:1–5, 8:

My brethren, do not hold your faith in our glorious Lord Jesus Christ with an attitude of personal favoritism. For if a man comes into your assembly with a gold ring and dressed in fine clothes, and there also comes in a poor man in dirty clothes, and you pay special attention to the one who is wearing the fine clothes, and say, "You sit here in a good place," and you say to the poor man, "You stand over there, or sit down by my footstool," have you not made distinctions among yourselves, and become judges with evil motives? Listen, my beloved brethren: did not God choose the poor of this world to be rich in faith and heirs of the kingdom which He promised to those who love Him? ... If, however, you are fulfilling the royal law according to the Scripture, "You shall love your neighbor as yourself," you are doing well.

I can't add much or state it any more clearly than that. Every person is a soul who deserves the same attention as the next. Look beyond their upbringing, living situation, or rough exterior. Whether they're a mess or they appear to have it together, they need God. Someone cared enough about you to connect with you and teach you about Christ. Pass it on.

Principle 5: Principle 5 is closely related to Principle 4. If you're going to reach people, you have to meet them where they are. Unless those are the same places you normally are, you're going to have to either expand your comfort zone or operate outside of it for a while. Of course, the prime example of identifying with sinners is Jesus, who left the glory of heaven to live among fallen humanity. "Therefore, He had to be made like His brethren in all things, so that He might become a merciful and faithful high priest in things pertaining to God, to make propitiation for the sins of the people" (Heb 2:17). It wasn't easy for Jesus to come to earth, but He did it because He loves us and wanted to save us. Sound familiar? *Loving people and wanting their salvation is being like Jesus.*

When I talk about meeting people where they are, I'm not thinking only of physical locations. I'm thinking of walking alongside them as they climb out of sin, or in their emotional and mental struggles, or with their spiritual questions. It's hard. It's messy. Many times, it's not any fun. But it is absolutely essential.

Paul understood this. He described the process at length in 1 Corinthians. He became a Jew to the Jews, a Gentile to the Gentiles, and weak to the weak. "I have become all things to all men, so that I may by all means save some. I do all things for the sake of the gospel, so that I may become a fellow partaker of it" (1 Cor 9:22–23). Sometimes this requires sacrificing your own comfort and even your own rights. Paul continued by outlining a situation where a believer is eating with an unbeliever and has to decide whether to eat meat sacrificed to idols. He concluded,

> Whether, then, you eat or drink or whatever you do, do all to the glory of God. Give no offense either to Jews or to Greeks or to the church of God; just as I also please all men in all things, not seeking my own profit but the profit of the many, so that they may be saved (1 Cor 10:31–33).

There may be people you don't want to talk to. They make you uncomfortable. Maybe they have even caused you harm. You are not responsible for what they have done, but you *are* responsible for what *you* do. "But if your enemy is hungry, feed him, and if he is thirsty, give him a drink" (Rom 12:20). Hebrews 13:2 says, "Do not neglect to show hospitality to strangers." Peter summed it all up:

> Keep your behavior excellent among the Gentiles, so that in the thing in which they slander you as evildoers, they may because of your good deeds, as they observe them, glorify God in the day of visitation (1 Pet 2:12).

Principle 6: Keep the goal in mind. Community outreach is a deliberate attempt to form connections by showing interest and care *for the purpose of drawing people to God*. You're working toward making those people your brothers and sisters in Christ. There's a whole lot of follow-up that has to happen to reach that goal. Paul's words to the Colossians should always run through our heads: "Conduct yourselves with wisdom toward outsiders, making the most of the opportunity. Let your speech always be with grace, as though seasoned with salt, so that you will know how you should respond to each person" (Col 4:5–6). Tell them *why* you're helping them. Invite them to study the Bible. Don't let the work stall out. Finish strong. Share the gospel.

Around 1980, the church of Christ in Alva, Oklahoma, operated a bus ministry in their community. They learned about a teenage girl named Rosanna who lived in town, and they added her to their route. When they would pull up, her dad would yell, "Rosanna, those church people are here again!" Her parents had no interest in it for themselves, but they let her go.

Rosanna decided to become a Christian. People from the church eventually convinced her parents to study the Bible with them, and after a lot of questioning and searching, her parents were baptized too. One of the men told her dad, "Dick, you're the last person I expected to become a Christian!" Rosanna went off to college and met a man who also converted to Christ. They had two daughters they raised in the church. Both of those daughters married believers.

I am telling you this story because Rosanna is my mother. I am here today, and three generations of my family know Christ, because of some Christians in Oklahoma who practiced community outreach and who would not give up on that family down the road. You never know what might happen because of that one person that you touch. Just try. God gives the increase. He did it in my life.

Remember Who You Are

DIANNE TAYS

Remember who you are. Several times as they were growing up, our children heard these words. As they went out the door on their way to meet their friends, their dad would tell them to be careful and to "remember who you are." What did he mean by this statement? One thing he meant was to remember that how they behaved affected not only them but their family. More importantly, how they behaved was a reflection of Christ. What would be the impact on our world if each of us remembered all the time who we are and whose we are?

1 John 2:6 reads, "Whoever claims to live in him must walk as Jesus did." Many of us sing a song in church titled "Footprints of Jesus" written by Mary B. C. Slade. The last line of the chorus reads, "We will follow the steps of Jesus where-e'er they go."[1] This world would be a much better place to live if we all followed in the footsteps of Jesus. Instead of just singing words, we should take the words that we sing and put them into action. Our world would be

a lot better place for all of us to live. School shootings, bullying, hunger, and homelessness would increasingly be things of the past. Our homes would be a better and safer place for all children as they grow up. Child abuse, spousal abuse, and elder abuse would no longer exist. Our friends, family, and neighbors would see us living a lifestyle that matches what we preach to them. We would be able to convert those around us by our example. We could convert residents of our city, our state, our country, and the entire world if only we did the things we talked about. This concept is so simple, and yet we have a hard time grasping it. In the book of Colossians, Paul, inspired by the Holy Spirit, tells us exactly how to behave to solve the problems we face.

In Colossians, Paul is writing to the Christians in Colosse. He has been made aware of problems that are infiltrating the church. In Colossians 2 he reminds these Christians that they are now "alive with Christ" (verse 13) and that they "died with Christ to the basic principles of this world" (verse 20). He then tells them to "set your hearts on things above" (Col 3:1). In Colossians 3:18–4:6 Paul proceeds to give these Christians instructions on how to behave as Christians. In verses 18–21 of chapter 3, Paul talks to family members about how they should treat each other. He tells wives to "submit to your husbands, as is fitting in the Lord." He talks to husbands: "Husbands, love your wives and do not be harsh with them." Then it is the children's turn in verse 20. "Children, obey your parents in everything, for this pleases the Lord." He speaks again to fathers saying to "not embitter your children, or they will become discouraged" (verse 21). Our families are the key to

Christian behavior, whether it is our physical family or our church family. How we treat each other is vitally important. Every family looks different and acts differently. Every member within the family is different. We have different interests, different personalities, and different attitudes. Therefore, we always need to have patience with each other. Before we react, think about if the difference is something that really matters. If it is not something against God's commands, maybe we could learn to accept that difference. Everything goes back to the love we have for each other, our attitude toward each other, and the love we have for the Lord. Family members irritate each other at times. Someone is playing his or her music too loud. Maybe we don't like the supper that has been prepared. Maybe our children's grades were lower than what we were expecting from them. We are tired from working all day. We are tired from school activities. We are tired from taking care of other people. We are upset because our lives didn't turn out the way we planned.

Christ didn't promise us that our lives would be perfect. Christians won't ever be perfect, but whether it is our physical family or our church family, we should always strive toward perfection. We should always be working towards a more Christ-like attitude. We should tell our families that we love them even when they are not perfect, even when they disappoint us. One day it will be us who make a mistake, and we will need others to forgive us. None of us grew up in a perfect home, with a perfect dad, a perfect mom, and perfect children. All families will have problems. We need to react to those problems as Christ would.

Each generation thinks the decades before them were the best. People in 2024 like to compare the world today to the 1950s and 1960s. We say that if we could only go back to those days everything would be so much better. We watch a television program and think that is what the real world is like. We think Mayberry was the perfect place to live. We like to remember the episode with Andy and Barney sitting on the front porch on a Sunday afternoon just taking it easy. No problems. Everything is great. If we remember the rest of the episode, things become very chaotic. There has never been a perfect place to live since the Garden of Eden. Every generation has had its own problems. The 1950s had the Korean War. The 1960s had the Vietnam War. There were riots, assassinations, and church bombings. Things were not perfect. In the '60s, we often heard sermons on how young people were "going to the dogs." Church leaders worried about who would lead the church after the older people were gone. They talked about people not wanting to be involved in the work of the church. Each of us can look back and think things were better in the past. After the passing of several years, we choose to forget the bad things and remember the good things. That is just human nature. If things in 2024 are not how we would like them to be, maybe we need to look at what we need to change about ourselves. If we didn't grow up with a Christian father or a Christian mother, then we should plan on being that Christian father or mother to our own children. Make sure they see us putting Christ first in our lives. Be an example to the children around us who don't have Christian parents. We complain about what is on television. Why don't we turn the television off? No one is forcing us to watch the shows that are on television or at movie theaters. Instead, we could play games together as a family. We could read books with our children. Read the Bible together more as a family. We could go for walks. If we don't like the lyrics of today's music, turn it off or turn the channel. We can find plenty of Christian music to listen to. We can sing church hymns in the car with our children on the way to baseball practice, band practice, or on the way to school. Paul mentions in Colossians 3:16, "Let the word of Christ dwell in you richly as you teach and admonish one another" as "you sing psalms, hymns, and spiritual songs with gratitude in your hearts to God." In Colossians 3:1 Paul says that we should always have our hearts and minds on things above. If we live a Christian life on this earth, then when we arrive in our home in Heaven, we will find that perfect family with God our Father, Christ our brother, and all our Christian brothers and sisters.

In Colossians 3:22–25, Paul deals with the slave and master relationships. Even though these verses are speaking to slaves and masters, we can apply them very easily to employees and employers. Simply substitute the word employees for slaves, and the word employers for masters. Colossians 3:22–23 would then read,

> Employees, obey your earthly employer in everything; and do it, not only when their eye is on you and to win their favor, but with sincerity of heart and reverence for the Lord. Work at it with all your heart, as working for the Lord, not for men.

Colossians 4:1 would read, "Employers, provide your employees with what is right and fair, because you know that you also have a Master in heaven." When we let the Lord direct us in the workplace, we will solve a lot of problems. Employees will no longer have to worry about how they are treated at work. Employers will no longer have to worry about absenteeism. Employees will show up when expected, ready to work to the best of their ability without complaining. None of us will be spreading rumors about our fellow workers, our supervisors, or our clients. Everybody would then have a great place to work. Imagine! We would practice the golden rule and treat each other as Christ would treat us.

Paul also tells us how to live a life for Christ. In Colossians 3:12–13, he tells us to

> clothe yourselves with compassion, kindness, humility, gentleness, and patience. Bear with each other and forgive whatever grievances you may have against each other. Forgive as the Lord forgave you.

In verses 14–15, Paul tells us to love each other and to let the peace of Christ rule us. In Colossians 4:2–3 he says for us to "devote yourselves to prayer." Think about these things. We should treat those around us with compassion, kindness, and gentleness. If we spent more time in prayer for our friends, our families, and our fellow workers, we would have less time to make mistakes. When we are praying for someone, it is hard to mistreat that person or talk about them. We would draw closer to God. Paul says to pray that "God will open a door for the message, so we may proclaim the mystery of Christ." He says for us to "be thankful." If we are thanking God for the people in our lives, it will be easier for us to overlook irritations. We are all different. We have different likes and dislikes. We think about things differently. We need to be able to talk and pray about our differences together. Sometimes we just need to "agree to disagree." We should never give up on anyone, even though we feel that they are a lost cause. God can be working in their lives even though we can't see it. We have all seen this happen with our friends and family members. It may take years, but we never know how the small seed that is planted is germinating within that person. One day that seed may sprout, and they will become a Christian.

Look at several people in the Bible who had sin in their lives, but later became followers of Christ. How did Jesus handle each situation? In John 4, Jesus meets the woman at the well. She had five previous husbands and was living with a man she was not married to. Jesus talked to her about worshiping God. He revealed to her that he was the Messiah. We know from John 4:39 that many in her town later believed because of her testimony. In John 8, a woman is caught in adultery. Christ didn't condemn her to death, but let her go with the instructions to not sin again. Even the apostles of Christ made mistakes. Thomas had doubts that Jesus had risen from the dead. He didn't believe in the resurrection until he saw the nail prints for himself. Peter, one of Christ's closest apostles, denied that he was a follower of Jesus three times. Christ forgave both Peter and Thomas. Both men lived the rest of their lives for Christ. In Acts 7, we read about Stephen, who was stoned for preaching the word. As he was dying, he asked God to forgive those who were stoning him. The greatest example of forgiveness was when our Savior asked God to forgive those who were crucifying him. Christ died on the cross for the sins of everyone who has ever lived. Our sins cost Jesus his life. If Christ can forgive all of us for our sins, we should be able to forgive each other for our offenses.

Paul's list of Christian behaviors continues in Colossians 4:5–6. He tells us to "be wise in the way you act toward outsiders," that we "make the most of every opportunity," and that our conversation is "always full of grace and seasoned with salt." These verses all come down to one thing. Every one of us should treat others in a manner that is pleasing to Christ. Christ doesn't care if we are poor or rich, if we are young or old, the employer or the employee, intelligent or uneducated. He doesn't care what country we were born in, what color our skin is, or what football team we cheer for. Those are things that we consider important. Those are things we let separate us from each other. Christ is only concerned about one thing. He wants us to follow him. He is concerned that we obey God's commands. He is concerned that we are baptized for the remission of our sins and that we live our lives dedicated to him.

The Christian life will not always be an easy life. The devil throws the unexpected at us. He tempts us and tries to make us fail. Our family members refuse to obey Christ. Our friends leave the church. We become angry or impatient with others. Our health fails us. We lose someone close to us and our faith is tested. Our job changes. No matter what happens to us, following Christ should always be our focus. We should continue to persevere.

As Mike did with our children, we need to remind ourselves several times a day who we are. We are children of God. We are the brothers and sisters of Christ. We are members of a great family, and we need to reflect Christ in that family wherever we are and whatever we are doing. Colossians 3:17 states, "And whatever you do, whether in word or deed, do it all in the name of the Lord Jesus, giving thanks to God the Father through him." Always remember whose you are.

For several years I have had the pleasure to work with Mechelle Thompson at Heritage Christian University. I have learned over those years that Mechelle is a great wife, mother, and grandmother. She is proud of her family. She is an example every day to all of us with her gentle speech and quiet demeanor. She is patient and loving and is always willing to help in any way that is needed. She has a great love for the students at Heritage Christian University. Mechelle is the Financial Aid Director at Heritage Christian and helps students with their financial situations daily. Mechelle is loved by her physical family, her spiritual family, and her Heritage Christian family. Most important of all, she has a great love for Christ. She is a Christian example to everyone, showing us all how to follow daily in the footsteps of Christ.

ENDNOTES

[1] Mary B. C. Slade, "Footprints of Jesus," *Songs of The Church*, (West Monroe, LA: Howard Publishers, 1971–1975), 113.

BIBLIOGRAPHY

NIV STUDY BIBLE (Fully Revised). Grand Rapids, MI: Zondervan. 1985, 1995, 2002.

Slade, Mary B. C. "Footprints of Jesus." *Songs of the Church*. West Monroe, LA: Howard Publishers, 1971–1975, 113.

"A New College with a New Idea"
THE BEGINNINGS OF HERITAGE CHRISTIAN UNIVERSITY[1]

BRAD MCKINNON

Heritage Christian University traces its roots to 1871 when T.B. Larimore opened Mars Hill Academy (College) on land inherited by his wife Esther Gresham Larimore. Located along Cox Creek near Florence, Alabama, Mars Hill Academy educated boys and girls, offering general education classes as well as specialized courses, including those in business and the arts. Scripture was emphasized at Mars Hill with daily chapel services required for each student. In time, Larimore began to focus primarily on equipping ministers and other Christian leaders for service in congregations associated with the American Restoration Movement.[2] These Bible students trained at Mars Hill established hundreds of congregations in Florence and surrounding communities in North Alabama and southern Tennessee. Initially housed in Larimore's home, the Academy closed in 1887 for Larimore to devote himself fully to evangelism. Reflecting on his school's legacy, Larimore observed,

Our school held its place on the hill and in the hearts and homes of its friends seventeen years—till it filled its mission and was mustered out of service that I might devote all my time and attention to evangelistic work.

Among those educated by Larimore at Mars Hill were notable restoration preachers F.D. Srygley and J.C. McQuiddy. The 12-room house was restored by the Associated Women's Organization of Mars Hill Bible School in 1971 and added to the National Register of Historic Places in 1974. The Larimores' house was destroyed by fire on July 19, 2022.[3]

Locally organized Christian education for the Churches of Christ resumed in 1947 when Lauderdale County Bible School (later Mars Hill Bible School), an elementary and secondary school, began on the site of the old Mars Hill Academy. Property for the school was purchased by William Wallace Alexander, a local physician, from T.B. Larimore's son, Virgil, who still resided on the land where his father had operated the original academy.[4] Mars Hill Bible School continues to provide preschool through high school education, having celebrated its 75th anniversary in 2022.

In November 1965, noting a shortage of preachers, several Shoals area church leaders, including Drake Macon, Barry Anderson, Albert Hill, and Robert Willis, proposed to the Mars Hill Board of Directors the establishment of a school to help prepare men for ministry. A steering committee, functioning under the Mars Hill board, quickly assumed responsibility for the promotion of the school, curriculum planning, and the selection of teachers.

Selected representatives for the school included Barry Anderson, Charles Coil, and Lois Behel. Supplementing the work of Mars Hill Bible School, the new T.B. Larimore School of Evangelists was seen as a restoration of the type of preacher training accomplished at Larimore's academy in the late 19th century. "Although T.B. Larimore is dead," Albert Hill observed, "his life, work, ambitions and desires live on in the hearts and lives of dedicated Christians who know, love, and appreciate this noble soldier of the cross."[5]

Opening in January 1966 with 70 students enrolled, the T.B. Larimore School of Evangelists followed the model of a non-credit Bible institute or preacher training school. The school offered courses designed to meet the needs of those who could not "expediently attend one of our [Christian] colleges." After operating in the spring and fall of 1966, the school's steering committee, at the direction of the Mars Hill Board of Directors, transitioned from an administrative function to an advisory one. There is no known record of the school meeting for classes after December 1966. Reflecting on the legacy of the School of Evangelists, Hill concluded, "The training school offered night courses only, one night a week, with much interest and accomplished great good but was discontinued." In 1967, to complement the ministry instruction that had already been offered in Florence, Harding University Graduate School of Religion located in Memphis, Tennessee, began offering extension classes for local ministers.[6]

The dream of providing localized higher education in the Shoals, designed specifically for the training of preachers, did not lay dormant for long. Before the end of 1967, plans were already underway to establish a private college in Florence, independent of Mars Hill, to prepare students for ministry. In 1968, those plans began taking shape when Malcolm Hill agreed to leave his work as preacher for the Forest Park congregation in greater Atlanta to become the inaugural president of the newly established Southeastern Institute (College) of the Bible in Florence. Inez Alexander, widow of William Wallace Alexander, donated land for a campus near the old T.B. Larimore home; local orthopedic surgeon, G.R. Melson, serving as chair of the Businessmen's Advisory Board, began efforts to establish an endowment for the school. Initial faculty included Malcolm Hill, Charles Coil, Bob Bryson, Lamar Plunket, Barry Anderson, A.R. Hill, and Albert Hill. Charles Coil also served as chair of the Preachers' Advisory Board. Founded in March 1968, Southeastern classes met for the first time in January 1969. The institute would include a three-year program offering bachelor's degrees in Sacred Literature and Religious Education. Initially, there were no plans to seek accreditation from secular or academic associations. Instead, the school would simply "offer a man the courses which he [would] need to fully equip him for the task of preaching the Word."[7]

Soon after Southeastern was established, some questions emerged regarding how the new school was being operated. Prominent minister Gus Nichols from Jasper, Alabama, chaired a meeting in July 1970 at the Eastwood Church of Christ in Florence to discuss a solution to the controversies. In October 1970, with the future of the college uncertain, the administration and board of Southeastern College of the Bible resigned, and a new board was elected. Those selected to serve on the reorganized Board of Directors were Ellis H. Coats, Howard Morris, Glenn Skipworth, Jimmy H. Parker, Vestal Shipman, James G. Smith, and Roger Peck. During this time of transition, Barry Anderson served as interim president of the school. Early in 1971, Charles Coil was selected by the new board as the second president of Southeastern College of the Bible.[8]

As president, Coil was empowered to establish a program unique among the Churches of Christ—the four-year Bible college. Neither a preacher training school nor a liberal arts college, the coeducational Bible college would have standardized admissions policies, academic calendar, and curriculum. In September 1971, Southeastern was renamed International Bible College. The administration explained that the name change was intended to distinguish the Florence school from an older institution in Birmingham bearing the same name. The new name would reflect the aspiration to train men and women for service in foreign countries and to develop "an international view." Having a new designation served a practical purpose for the college as well by helping provide the administration the fresh start it desired to move beyond the disputes of the past and onward as "a new college with a new idea."[9] In 1989, after serving eighteen years as the college's chief administrator, Charles Coil announced his resignation as president of International Bible College. He continued to serve as chancellor until his death in 1994. IBC alumnus, Dennis Jones, succeeded Coil as the institution's third president, taking office on January 1, 1990.[10] To help meet the need for advanced education for ministers and church leaders, a graduate program offering Master of Ministry and Master of Arts degrees was added in 2000. In January 2001, the institution changed its name to Heritage Christian University to reflect its status as a graduate-degree-granting institution and in August 2001, the first graduates were awarded master's degrees. The university initiated a Master of Divinity program with an emphasis on small church growth in 2011. The retirement of Dennis Jones as president was announced in April 2017 and in December of that year, HCU's Board of Directors selected W. Kirk Brothers as the university's fourth president. On Founders Day, March 9, 2023, the university celebrated its 55th anniversary.[11]

ENDNOTES

[1] I would like to first acknowledge the decades-long commitment my colleague Mechelle Thompson has made to the mission of Heritage Christian University. She has blessed countless students through the years and has been an anchor for the HCU administration, faculty, and staff through her work in the Office of Financial Aid where she currently serves as director. I would also like to recognize those who have worked diligently through the years to tell the important story of Heritage Christian University. Particularly noteworthy are Vernon Shuffett, whose monograph entitled *As the Waters Cover the Sea: Heritage Christian University (The International Bible College Era)* established an important foundation from which to understand the university's history, and my colleague Wayne Kilpatrick, Emeritus Professor of Church History at HCU, whose tire-

less commitment to preserving voices from the past has inspired many.

² Emma Page Larimore, *Life, Letters, and Sermons of T.B. Larimore* (Nashville: Gospel Advocate, 1931), 106–107; Mars Hill Academy, Advertisement, January 21, 1874, *Florence Times-Journal*; Larimore, *Life, Letters, and Sermons of T.B. Larimore*, 113.

³ "Mars Hill's Storied History," Mars Hill Bible School, accessed December 14, 2015, http://www.mhbs.org/index.php/aboutus/our-history; "National Register of Historic Places Inventory – Nomination Form," United States Department of the Interior, National Park Service, accessed August 30, 2016, http://npgallery.nps.gov/pdfhost/docs/NRHP/Text/74000416.pdf; Tom Smith, "Officials searching for cause of Larimore Home fire," TimesDaily (Florence, AL), July 20, 2018, accessed Dec 11, 2023. https://www.timesdaily.com/news/ officials-searching-for-cause-of-larimore-home-fire/article_6642f921-8b9d-5b04-bfed-9da3d5df4346.html.

⁴ Douglas A. Foster, "Mars Hill Bible School," in *The Encyclopedia of the Stone-Campbell Movement*, ed. Douglas A. Foster, Paul M. Blowers, Anthony L. Dunnavant, and D. Newell Williams (Grand Rapids: Eerdmans, 2004), 503; "Mars Hill's Storied History."

⁵ Albert Hill, "T.B. Larimore School of Evangelists," *Gospel Advocate* 107, no. 47 (November 25, 1965): 761; Board of Directors Meeting Minutes, November 9, 1965, Board of Directors Records, Mars Hill Bible School, Florence, AL; T.B. Larimore School of Evangelists, Brochure (Florence, AL: Mars Hill Bible School, 1966); Albert Hill, "T.B. Larimore School of Evangelists," 761.

⁶ Board of Directors Meeting Minutes, December 22, 1966, Board of Directors Records, Mars Hill Bible School, Florence, AL; Albert Hill, "Southeastern Institute of the Bible," *Gospel Defender* 10, no. 4 (March 1969): 1; Ellis H. Coats (former IBC board member) in conversation with the author, January 14, 2016.

⁷ Albert Hill, "Southeastern Institute of the Bible," *Gospel Advocate* 110, no. 24 (June 13, 1968): 375; Southeastern Institute of the Bible, "Certificate of Incorporation," March 9, 1968; Albert Hill, "Southeastern Institute of the Bible," *Gospel Defender* 10, no. 4 (March 1969): 1.

⁸ Charles Coil, O'Neal E. Smelser, Ellis H. Coats, Jerry Humphries, Albert Hill, Malcolm L. Hill (unsigned), and Barry L. Anderson to Whom It May Concern, 1 August 1974, Heritage Christian University Archives, Overton Memorial Library; Board of Directors Meeting Minutes, October 5, 1970, Board of Directors Records, Southeastern College of the Bible, Florence, AL; Southeastern College of the Bible, "Charles Coil Named President of Southeastern Bible College," news release, February 1, 1971.

⁹ Charles Coil, "A Statement of Purpose from the President of Southeastern College of the Bible," Heritage Christian University Archives, Overton Memorial Library; Board of Directors Meeting Minutes, August 24, 1971, Board of Directors Records, Southeastern College of the Bible, Florence, AL; Southeastern College of the Bible, "Local College Changes Name," news release, September 17, 1971; "A New College with a New Idea," advertisement, *Gospel Advocate* 113, no. 32 (August 12, 1971).

¹⁰ Board of Directors Meeting Minutes, September 28, 1989, Board of Directors Records, International Bible

College, Florence, AL; Board of Directors Meeting Minutes, September 28, 1989, Board of Directors Records, International Bible College, Florence, AL.

[11] Board of Directors Meeting Minutes, April 28, 2000, Board of Directors Records, International Bible College, Florence, AL; Lucille Prince, "Celebrating the Heritage," *TimesDaily* (Florence, AL), January 27, 2001; Board of Directors Meeting Minutes, August 27, 2011, Board of Directors Records, Heritage Christian University, Florence, AL; "Announcement of Retirement," news release, April 7, 2017; "University Board Names Brothers Next President," news release, December 21, 2017.

The Call of Wisdom
PROVERBS 1:20-33
LUCAS SUDDRETH

Many years ago when my wife and I were newlyweds, we took a vacation to New Orleans, Louisiana. At the time we were living in Florence, Alabama, and this was our first big trip away from home and family. We were nervous but excited. We spent our first day in the French Quarter and fell in love with the atmosphere, cuisine, and architecture. By the end of the week, we had explored several different neighborhoods, thoroughly enjoyed our time, and promised ourselves we would come back soon.

Even though we had a great time in New Orleans, the most memorable part of the trip happened after our return to Florence. I was working at Heritage Christian University, and there, I recounted to Mechelle Thompson all the activities and experiences we had. At one point, I mentioned how more than a few individuals were asking for money, and I admitted that I didn't feel comfortable giving out money because I was unsure if they would spend it wisely. It was at that point that Mechelle blessed me with a piece of wisdom that I pray will stay with me for the rest of my life. She said something to this effect:

> Lucas, you will never know exactly what these individuals do with the money you give them. Some will use it wisely, and others will not. Instead, when someone asks you for assistance, give to them what you can and let God handle the rest.

At that moment, I saw the wisdom of Mechelle's words. It caused me to completely reexamine my approach to helping others. I was blessed that day to receive some wisdom from Mechelle, and to see that she had already sought after wisdom herself and found it. Of course, on that day, I merely saw a glimpse of her wisdom, but there were other instances in our time working together that confirmed it. This is why when I read the words of Proverbs 8:34–35, I think of her. Here, it says, *"Blessed is the one who listens to me [wisdom], watching daily at my gates, waiting beside my doors. For whoever finds me finds life and obtains favor from the LORD."*[1] Mechelle has lived, and will continue to live, a joy-filled life because she has heeded wisdom's call and found favor from the Lord. The following words are written in honor of her.

The book of Proverbs belongs to the genre called wisdom literature. Books in this category are known for their parables or short statements about righteous living, such as truthfulness, justice, and order, among other things.[2] The post-exilic period was a time when large amounts of wisdom literature were being produced and collected in Israel. But, prior to this, wisdom writings were being penned and dispersed across the ancient world for several millennia.[3] Some of the earliest records date from the 3rd millennium BC in the regions of Egypt and Mesopotamia.[4] In fact, Stephen himself speaks of Egyptian wisdom in Acts 7:22, giving it great significance when he says, "*Moses was instructed in all the wisdom of the Egyptians, and he was mighty in his words and deeds.*" While wisdom literature comes from many different regions and periods of time, they share a common goal—for the reader to seek after and attain the knowledge and understanding that comes from wisdom.

In the ancient Israelite book of Proverbs, wisdom is uniquely personified as a woman. Considering the first eight chapters of the book are from the perspective of a father giving advice to his son, it is sensible that the father would personify wisdom in this way. He is trying to express the desire the son should have for wisdom, describing her as "*more precious than jewels,*" and encouraging him to "*hold her fast.*"[5]

The reader is first introduced to wisdom in Proverbs 1:20–33. She is personified not as a meek and shy child, but as a strong and confident woman. Therefore, she is often referred to as *Lady Wisdom* and will be called as such for the remainder of this article. Verses 20–23 introduce her in this way,

> Wisdom cries aloud in the street,
> in the markets she raises her voice;
> at the head of the noisy streets she
>   cries out;
> at the entrance of the city gates she speaks:

> "How long, O simple ones, will you love being simple?
> How long will scoffers delight in their scoffing
> and fools hate knowledge?
> If you turn at my reproof,
> behold, I will pour out my spirit to you;
> I will make my words known to you.

Again, one sees that wisdom is not a meek child but a confident woman. In the streets and busy intersections, in the central marketplaces and the outer gates, she makes her plea. Her words are not for the elite or select few; the old or successful. Her plea in this moment is to the פֶּתִי (*peti*) or the young, naïve, and simple young men who lack wisdom.[6] She is not trying to demean or shame them for being in their current state, for every person begins life in a state of naïveté and youthfulness. Instead, she calls them to leave their current state, lacking in wisdom, and heed her call. Her message is a mild correction, or reproof, meant to wake them up to their situation and create a desire to follow her. For in Proverbs, there are only two paths to take in this life—the path of wisdom or the path of folly.[7] Her words are a warning that, should they ignore her call, the naïve will continue down the path of the simple, which terminates at the house of Lady Folly—the entrance to Sheol.[8] However, it is not too late. Should they heed Lady Wisdom's call, she will bring them wisdom and understanding, long life and riches, peace and blessedness.[9]

While Lady Wisdom largely addresses the naïve throughout the Proverbs, there are two additional groups mentioned in her plea—the scoffer and the fool. Both are related to the naïve in that they lack wisdom but have moved past being merely young and simple, becoming openly derisive and arrogant (the scoffer), or obstinate and senseless (the fool) toward wisdom and her call. These individuals have chosen the path of folly and, because of their arrogance and senselessness, have no intention of turning back. Nonetheless, Lady Wisdom still calls to them, urging them to turn at her correction, receive her spirit (frame of mind)[10], and to gain her words (knowledge and understanding).

Even though Lady Wisdom makes her call throughout the city, even though she appeals to the trio (the naïve, the scoffer, and the fool), she knows they have not listened to her words. She has alerted them to their situation and the path they are traveling. She has tried to cultivate a desire within them for wisdom. But the three groups are not swayed by her minor reproof. Therefore, she delivers a more powerful rebuke in verses 24–30 toward those who have *"refused to listen"* and *"ignored my counsel."*[11] Specifically, in verses 26–27, she says,

> I also will laugh at your calamity;
> I will mock when terror strikes you,
> when terror strikes you like a storm
> and your calamity comes like a whirlwind,
> when distress and anguish come upon you.

When hearing these words for the first time, many readers are shocked at Lady Wisdom's response. With a cursory glance, it appears vindictive that she would respond with laughter and mockery at someone's downfall. However, looking at the passage as a whole, this is the part of her plea that challenges their youthful sense of strength and invincibility, a topic addressed in the verses immediately preceding this speech of Lady Wisdom.[12] She uses strong and violent imagery in order to catch their attention for she is now speaking in their language. The purpose is to give them a reason to pause and consider abandoning their current path of foolishness. According to Michael Fox in his commentary on Proverbs, "Wisdom does not, strictly speaking, vow or predict that disaster will overtake the fools; she *assumes* it."[13] This reinforces the theme in Proverbs that the path of folly leads to calamity and even death for individuals who choose to follow it.[14] Lady Wisdom affirms this belief when speaking of the "terror," "calamity," "distress," and "anguish" found on the path of foolishness. These are words often used in apocalyptic literature to describe impending doom.[15] Thus, Lady Wisdom will laugh at and mock the trio because they could have avoided this fate if they had only listened to her call, taken her outstretched hand, heeded her counsel, or obeyed her reproof.[16] Instead, they will take the path of foolishness to their doom.

The great tragedy in these final moments is that the trio will finally realize the error of their ways. In their distress, they will call out to her, but it will be too late. Lady Wisdom describes the ordeal in verses 28–32:

> Then they will call upon me, but I will not answer;

THE CALL OF WISDOM

> they will seek me diligently but will not
>   find me.
> therefore they shall eat the fruit of
>   their way,
> and have their fill of their own devices.
> For the simple are killed by their turning
>   away,
> and the complacency of fools destroys them;
> but whoever listens to me will dwell secure
> and will be at ease, without dread of disaster.

For much of their lives, Lady Wisdom has been calling to this trio. But now that they have followed the path of foolishness and arrived at Lady Folly's house, wisdom's call goes silent. In that silence, the trio will remember Lady Wisdom's words and all that she promised if they would only heed her call. In desperation, they will finally respond to her words; they will now call to her! But they will soon grasp the reason for her silence—she is gone.

While it may seem harsh for Lady Wisdom to leave the trio at such a critical point in their lives, she explains why their call will go unanswered. In verses 31–32, she says they must "*eat the fruit of their way, and have their fill of their own devices.*" Lady Wisdom believes they are getting their just rewards for their actions. As the saying goes, they have made their bed and must now lie in it. People cannot walk the path of folly all their lives and then expect wisdom to save them in their final moments. She responds in this way because one of her attributes is justice, and it is part of the knowledge and understanding she imparts to make one wise. In Proverbs 1:3, wisdom gives "*instruction in wise deal-*

ing, in righteousness, justice, and equity." Therefore, it is because of her justice that she leaves the trio to their own devices. They have walked the path of destruction and, thus, having reached its terminus, will now meet their doom.

For many in today's modern culture, the words of Lady Wisdom are harsh, sardonic, and judgmental. Anyone in our culture trying to publish these words would most likely struggle to find a publisher and suffer from low sales. It is no surprise that modern individuals do not appreciate such sharp speech. It is incredibly personal, piercing the reader to the core. But the reader must remember the purpose of this speech. Lady Wisdom is trying to shake the naïve, the scoffer, and the fool to their core. She attempts to grab their attention with strong words because soft words appear weak to the trio. She goes to the extreme in her speech, even laughing at others' calamity so that they might be awakened to the reality of their folly. While she may not say it outright, she does this because she cares for them.[17]

With this in mind, the final statement of Lady Wisdom is found in verse 33, where she says, *"But whoever listens to me will dwell secure and will be at ease, without dread of disaster.*" While many have already made their choice by taking the path of foolishness, Lady Wisdom closes her speech with a word of hope. Even though her call will go unheeded by many, she makes her final plea. She says to all, come and dwell with me, for here you will be secure and at ease.

ENDNOTES

[1] All scripture is taken from the English Standard Version (2016).

[2] Daniel Estes, *Hear, My Son*, New Studies in Biblical Theology (Grand Rapids: Eerdmans, 1997), 26.

[3] Roland E. Murphy, "Wisdom in the OT," *AYBD* 6 (New Haven: Yale University Press, 2008), 921, 929.

[4] Murphy, "Wisdom in the OT," 921, 929.

[5] Proverbs 2:15, 18.

[6] Also, Proverbs 8:5, 9:6.

[7] Proverbs 1:15; 2:13, 18, 20; 3:17; 4:14; 5:5; 7:25; 8:20.

[8] Proverbs 7:27.

[9] Proverbs 3:13–18.

[10] "רוּחַ," HALOT, 3:1199.

[11] Proverbs 1:24, 25.

[12] Proverbs 1:10–19.

[13] Michael V. Fox, *Proverbs 1–9*, The Anchor Yale Bible (New Haven: Yale University Press, 1974), 101.

[14] See also Proverbs 1:10–19; 2:18; 5:5; 7:27.

[15] Roland E. Murphy, *Proverbs*, WBC 22 (Nashville: Thomas Nelson, 1998), 11.

[16] Proverbs 1:24–25.

[17] Proverbs 4:6.

WORKS CITED

Estes, Daniel. *Hear, My Son*. New Studies in Biblical Theology. Grand Rapids: Eerdmans, 1997.

Fox, Michael V. *Proverbs 1–9*. The Anchor Yale Bible. New Haven: Yale University Press, 1974.

Koehler, Ludwig, Walter Baumgartner, and M. E. J. Richardson, eds. *The Hebrew and Aramaic Lexicon of the Old Testament*. 5 vols. Leiden: Brill, 2000.

Murphy, Roland E. *Proverbs*. WBC 22. Nashville: Thomas Nelson, 1998.

Murphy, Roland E., Freedman, David Noel, eds. *The Anchor Yale Bible Dictionary*. 6 vols. New Haven: Yale University Press, 2008.

The Apostle Who Lived

ED GALLAGHER

> But now the time has come to go away. I go to die, and you to live; but which of us goes to the better lot, is known to none but God.
>
> —Socrates[1]

It is a pleasure to offer this sermon in honor of Mechelle Thompson, who provides a living example of someone honoring God through her life and, indeed, through how she has faced life-threatening situations. May we learn from her example.

One time Peter got put in prison in Jerusalem during the time of Passover. The story is told in Acts 12. The year was probably AD 44. The text says that it was King Herod who put him in prison. Now, there are various Herods mentioned in the New Testament. This Herod in Acts 12 is not the most famous Herod, the one who killed the babies of Bethlehem (Matt 2:16). That was Herod the Great, the first in the line of Herods. Our Herod in Acts 12 is called

Herod Agrippa, and he is the grandson of Herod the Great. Later on in Acts, Paul will meet another king whom the biblical text calls Agrippa (Acts 25–26), who is the son of the Herod Agrippa in Acts 12. Historians call the father Herod Agrippa I and the son Herod Agrippa II.

Herod Agrippa I put Peter in prison with the plan to execute him after Passover and the days of unleavened bread (Acts 12:4). But on the night before the scheduled execution, an angel showed up in the prison and set Peter free. God sent an angel to save Peter's life, to rescue him from certain death. Our God can do things like that. Once Peter was out of the prison, he went to the house of Mary, mother of John Mark, where the church had gathered to pray on Peter's behalf. You remember what happened next. Peter knocked on the door and announced that he had been released. Rhoda the servant was so excited to tell everyone that she forgot to let Peter in. Nobody believed Rhoda; they thought it must have been his angel (Acts 12:15), whatever that means. When Peter finally got into the house, he reported about his escape and left.

We know what year all this happened because of the next event narrated in the chapter: Herod Agrippa I died. According to Josephus, Agrippa I died in the year AD 44.[2] The story Luke tells about this death contains the memorable and potentially confusing wording that the king "was eaten by worms and breathed his last" (Acts 12:23). We sometimes say that once a person has died, he becomes worm food, but Acts says that the worms were eating Agrippa before he died. Of course, that sometimes happens. The ancient Greek historian Herodotus described something similar about Queen Pheretima in

Libya in the sixth century BC: "she died a horrible death, her body seething with worms while she was still alive" (4.205).[3] According to Luke, the judgment of God came upon this King Herod for his arrogance, illustrated in his futile attempt to kill one of the Lord's apostles.

Acts 12 is a story of liberation. It shows us the power of God, who is able to rescue from death. This story encourages us as readers to recognize that a hopeless situation is brimming with hope as long as we trust in the God who loves us and can cause everything to work out for our benefit (Rom 8:28).

This story is not the only time that Peter had seen the Lord rescue someone from death. During his ministry in Galilee, Jesus sometimes raised up people who had already died. One time there was a synagogue leader named Jairus who approached Jesus asking for help for his sick daughter. By the time Jesus got to Jairus's house, the report was already circulating about the girl's death. Jesus's response to this report? "Do not fear, only believe" (Mark 5:36). Jesus went into the girl's room and simply said, "Talitha cum" (5:41)—and she got up! Peter was there, he heard those words from Jesus's mouth, he saw the girl rise and eat. Do you remember who else was in that room at the time? Aside from the girl's parents, it was only Peter, James, and John.

We sometimes see this trio of apostles granted special privileges, not enjoyed by the other apostles. These were the three on the mount of transfiguration, who witnessed Jesus glowing and talking with Moses and Elijah (Mark 9:2–8). Later, in what seems like the moment of Jesus's greatest need, it was Peter and James and John with him in the garden of Gethsemane (Mark 15:32–42). While all twelve apostles had their mission from Jesus, it seems like the Big Three were an especially important group with an unusually intimate relationship with Jesus.

Peter, the rock (John 1:42).

James and John, the sons of thunder (Mark 3:17).

No doubt Jesus had big plans for these three special apostles, some sort of special project.

The Gospels record some stories that involve just James and John without Peter. It was these two brothers who suggested to Jesus that they could call fire down from heaven against some rude Samaritans. Sons of thunder. Jesus rolled his eyes (Luke 9:51–55). It was also James and John (Mark 10:35–40)—or, actually, their mother (Matt 20:20–28)—who asked for the best seats in the kingdom of God, on the right and left of the Messiah. This time, Jesus did not roll his eyes but asked a question: "Are you able to drink the cup that I drink, or be baptized with the baptism with which I am baptized?" (Mark 10:38). James and John answered confidently, "yes, we can do that!" Did they know what they were talking about? We can be sure that they did not know the full import of their words. Jesus actually told them, "You do not know what you are asking" (10:38). But did they realize that the cup Jesus mentioned, and the baptism, had to do with suffering? I'm not sure, maybe. They may have thought that they were proclaiming their readiness to serve on the front lines in the coming war, to put themselves in dangerous situations for the kingdom of God. They probably did not realize that there would be no battle against Rome or any earthly foe. But they may have thought that they had signed up for some degree of suffering. And Jesus told them that they were right about that. "The cup that I drink you will drink; and with the baptism with which I am baptized, you will be baptized" (10:39). Jesus would endure suffering, and so would James and John.

Acts 12 does not start with King Herod putting Peter in prison. It starts with Herod imprisoning James, the brother of John. In prison is one of the sons of thunder, one of the Big Three apostles. There is no rescue plan from God, no miraculous escape. Instead, Herod "had James, the brother of John, killed with the sword" (Acts 12:2). Peter would be saved by a miracle, but not James. Why the one and not the other? Luke does not tell us.

When Peter was imprisoned, Christians gathered to pray in the house of one of their members. They asked God to spare the life of this beloved leader. Do you think that the church did the same for James? When James was taken by the authorities, do you think the Christians prayed for him, too? What did they pray? Of course, we don't know the words of their prayer, but let me offer a suggestion by reminding you about an incident that James witnessed.

One of those occasions when the Big Three were alone with Jesus was in Gethsemane. The way Mark tells the story (perhaps based on the memories of Peter),[4] the Big Three were having trouble staying awake. It was late at night. Even if they hadn't fallen asleep, I'm not sure they were close enough to overhear what Jesus prayed, but somehow people found out what the Lord prayed in the garden because it's reported in all three of the Synoptic Gospels (Matt 26:39; Mark 14:36; Luke 22:42): "Let this cup pass from me; yet not what I will, but your will be done."

Do you think it's possible that—assuming the church gathered to pray for James after his arrest—they reflected on Jesus's prayer in the garden? James had probably told them many times about what he witnessed that night, about his shame at falling asleep in that hour, about how he wished he had realized at the time the significance of the events he was experiencing, and about Jesus's prayer. James had probably said that when it came to his own hour of death, he hoped he would face death in the same way Jesus did. Do you think it's possible that the church prayed for James just as Jesus prayed in the garden, so that they asked God to let this cup pass from the apostle, if it be God's will—and if it be not God's will, but if rather God will that James should drink the cup to the dregs, perhaps the church prayed that James would show himself worthy of imitating Jesus through a brave and noble death.

We usually recoil from death, try to prevent it by every means possible, even though we all know that it's coming. Sometimes we encounter people who seem to stare at death and—far from recoiling at it—endeavor to die in a particular fashion. There's a moment in the novel *Dracula* when Arthur Holmwood (by now, Lord Godalming) is asked to give his beloved Lucy Westenra a transfusion of blood. Poor Lucy has been experiencing a repeated and mysterious loss of blood. Only Abraham Van Helsing seems to have any idea of how the blood was leaving her body, and what those two tiny pinprick holes on the side of her neck might have to do with it. At any rate, she needs blood immediately, and Van Helsing asks Arthur to supply the blood. Arthur answers, "If you only knew how gladly I would die for her."[5]

We can think of other examples. I believe that not every state has a designated state hero, but the state hero of Connecticut is a man named Nathan Hale. At age 21, he was arrested by the British as an American spy during the early period of the Revolutionary War. When he was hanged on September 22, 1776, his last words were reported as, "I only regret that I have but one life to lose for my country."

There are plenty of examples of noble deaths in religion as well. Near the end of the second century AD, the Christian author Tertullian wrote in his *Apology* (ch. 50), "The blood of the martyrs is the seed of the church," meaning that Christians endure death in so noble a fashion that it actually attracts people to this illegal religion. The writer of Hebrews mentioned people who accepted death in this way: "Others were tortured, refusing to accept release, in order to obtain a better resurrection" (Heb 11:35). The author here is probably thinking of the Maccabean martyrs, who had experienced terrible suffering and death about two centuries before Jesus was killed. We know the story of these martyrs from the apocryphal book of 2 Maccabees, probably written in the second century BC. The wicked king Antiochus Epiphanes tried to force Jews to abandon their law, threatened death if they didn't eat pork. Of course, some gave in, abandoned their faith to preserve their earthly lives. But 2 Maccabees 7 describes a family of seven brothers and their mother who "were tortured, refusing to accept release, in order to obtain a better resurrection." Each brother, and their mother, made a speech, declaring their resolve to endure the worst suffering the Greek tyrant could offer—and the chapter describes some pretty awful punishments. They basically said, like Arthur Holmwood, "If you only knew how gladly we would die for our God," or like Nathan Hale, "I only regret that I have but one life to lose for my Lord."

I am not sure how James faced his death. Did he make a speech? Did he face it bravely? Luke does not say. The fourth-century church historian Eusebius told a story about James going to his death, a story in which James did make a speech, bravely declaring the name of Christ, such a moving speech that the soldier guarding him gained the courage to reveal that he himself was also a Christian, and the two marched out together and were both executed (*Ecclesiastical History* 2.9). Should we trust that story? Is that close to the way it happened? Did James cower in fear before the executioner, or did he welcome the chance to prove his faith in the way that martyrs before and after him did?

To ask the question is to encounter an obvious answer. Surely this son of thunder did not shrink in fear. I bet that at the moment of his death, James remembered having been on the mountain, one of the privileged few, amazed at the bright light emanating from his Lord, standing there with Moses and Elijah. I'm sure as he walked toward the executioner, James remembered the instructions of Jesus, if you would be my disciple, you will take up your cross (Mark 8:34). I bet he remembered his younger and more impetuous self, and that once (or was it more than once?) he had the audacity to ask for the best seats in the kingdom. And I bet he remembered how Jesus answered this request with a question about drinking a cup and about a kind of baptism—a question to which he had confidently asserted, "Yes! I will drink that cup! I will receive that baptism!" Walking toward the executioner, he finally realized the significance of those words, and Jesus's reply, "You will drink that cup. You will receive that baptism." Luke does not tell us how James felt in that moment, but I bet he remembered the words of Jesus and saw his death as an opportunity to fully imitate his master, to be a true disciple of Jesus, to glorify God. "If you only knew how gladly I would die for him."

That makes me wonder how Peter felt to be rescued.

I've never been in combat, never been in a war zone, never been a part of the military. I understand from TV and movies that soldiers sometimes experience something called survivor's guilt. (There's a Wikipedia page on the condition.) Out of the many great World War II movies, one of the greatest is called *The Best Years of Our Lives* (1946), starring Fredric March and others. It tells the story of some WWII veterans who return from war and have trouble adjusting to "normal" life, in part because it seemed so pointless after what they had just experienced, in part because of the physical toll the war took on them, and in large measure because they wonder why they survived to live this easy and comfortable life while so many of their friends had died in battle. Why was I chosen to live? Near the end of *Les Miserables*, Marius sings these words:

> *Oh my friends, my friends forgive me*
> *That I live and you are gone*
> *There's a grief that can't be spoken*
> *There's a pain goes on and on.*[6]

How did Peter feel about the miraculous rescue he enjoyed after witnessing his dear friend and fellow apostle, co-member of the Big Three, die such a cruel and noble death? Peter had no doubt joined with others and prayed for James, prayed for his release, prayed for God's will to be done no matter what. James was given an opportunity denied Peter by that angel. Did Peter feel guilty for living?

The most famous speech in American history contains this passage:

> It is for us the living rather to be dedicated here to the unfinished work which they who fought here have thus far so nobly advanced. It is rather for us to be here dedicated to the great task remaining before us—that from these honored dead we take increased devotion to that cause for which they gave the last full measure of devotion—that we here highly resolve that these dead shall not have died in vain.

For present purposes I am not so interested in "government of the people, by the people, for the people," but I quote Lincoln for what he says about the purpose of living after so many have died. "It is for us the living rather to be dedicated here to the unfinished work which they who fought here have thus far so nobly advanced." The apostle James was given the opportunity—and seized it!—to so nobly advance the kingdom of God. Peter was not given that same opportunity in Acts 12. What should he do? Be dedicated to the unfinished work.

We are in the position of Peter. God has allowed us to live to this point. What do we do with that? Be dedicated to the unfinished work until we are granted the privilege of honoring God through our deaths. James enjoyed that privilege in Acts 12. Peter would have to wait. For now, his great task was to honor God with his life.

According to a popular report, George Washington once said to a young lieutenant colonel who had dreams of dying for the patriot cause during the Revolutionary War: "Dying is easy, young man; living is harder." James had the privilege of honoring God through his death. Peter now had the burden of honoring God through his life. We share that burden. Until that day when God permits us to imitate James, he calls on us to imitate the apostle who lived.

ENDNOTES

[1] Socrates, in Plato, *Apology* 42a (the very last words of the *Apology*). The translation is from Harold North Fowler, *Plato*, vol. 1, Loeb Classical Library (Cambridge, MA: Harvard University Press, 1914), 145.

[2] Of course, Josephus does not use our dating system; see the report of Agrippa's reign at *Antiquities* 19.351–52.

[3] Other, even more explicit (and gross) examples can be found at 2 Maccabees 9:9 (Antiochus IV Epiphanes); Eusebius, *Ecclesiastical History* 8.16.4 (Galerius). Eusebius (*Eccl. Hist.* 2.10) described the death of Agrippa, citing Josephus by name. He had previously (*Hist. eccl.* 2.4) reported the appointment of Agrippa by Caligula. On the death of Herod the Great, see Josephus, *War* 1.656, who includes worms among a variety of other ailments. In regard to Agrippa I, Josephus does not mention worms, but he does

mention a pain in the abdomen, and he says that God brought about Agrippa's death in part because the people addressed Agrippa as a god and Agrippa failed to rebuke them (*Antiquities* 19.345–50).

[4] According to early Christian tradition; see Eusebius, *Ecclesiastical History* 2.15.1–2.

[5] Bram Stoker, *Dracula* (1895), chapter 10.

[5] From the song "Empty Chairs at Tables."

Maturity in Ministry

ANDREW PHILLIPS

If you preach or teach regularly, the challenge is familiar. You are asked to speak on a certain topic or asked to address a specific issue in class, and your initial response is to feel unqualified. One of the recent assignments I received had that effect on me. I was asked to address the subject of maturity in ministry. While this is a topic of vital importance, tackling it is a daunting task. I might feel differently if I handled every ministry challenge with maturity, but I can still think of many ways that I need to mature and areas of my ministry that could use improvement.

On the other hand, one of the blessings I have experienced in my life is the chance to spend time around and work with excellent leaders. I have had the privilege of watching my father minister to others and learning from his example and advice. I have had the opportunity to work alongside other ministers who have taught me a great deal, and I have benefitted from teachers who have encouraged, challenged, and inspired me. I don't come to this topic as an experienced expert who knows exactly what a mature ministry looks like in every situation. Instead, I try to identify and address specific qualities of mature ministry that I have observed in the lives of effective ministers. These are attributes I aspire to in my own ministry.[1]

MATURITY IN MINISTRY PRIORITIZES STUDY WITHOUT SACRIFICING ACTIVITY.

One of the most influential pieces of writing I read in school was a short work by Jack Lewis entitled, "The Ministry of Study." He challenged those preparing for ministry to consider their study as a ministry rendered to the Lord. When discussing the temptation for a minister to say there is no time for study, Lewis wrote:

> Though they affirm personal willingness to go where the Lord would have them go, to make whatever sacrifices may be needed, and to face untold dangers if they arise, for many men the discipline of the study desk is just not what they have in mind...The man who cannot take time to prepare himself is dooming himself to a lifetime of frustration.[2]

In his essay, Lewis reminds us that study is not a chore we are obligated to do so that we can get around to doing ministry. Study is ministry. Yet we continue to face distractions in our study time. It has never been easier for a minister to spend time on the computer and feel like he is working, only to realize that after reading a few e-mails, checking social media accounts, and then being distracted by a couple of articles, not much has been accomplished. Our devices have given us access to books in electronic formats, which means we can study anywhere. But those same devices usually also show us push notifications, text messages, and other distractions. Access to information around the world is valuable, yet after scanning through an article, we might feel more confident about our knowledge in a specific area than we should.

Studying is vital. There is simply no substitute for deep study of a subject. Students spend years in school to become physicians, for example, and that education includes a tremendous amount of reading, memorization, and study. That training is vital because the best thing they can do for their patients is to be prepared and capable when they are needed. Rushing through that time of study might allow them to see patients sooner, but they would not be as equipped to give people what they needed.

Carving out time to study is important and difficult, especially because it requires discipline in our scheduling. In ministry, activity receives an immediate reward. When we visit someone in the hospital, we can see that person's face light up when we enter the room. At a funeral visitation, we can sense the appreciation for our presence. But when we are sitting in a quiet place studying, the feedback is not immediate. Sure, we appreciate that time when we are standing in front of a congregation preaching, but when we are doing the work of study, that moment is usually days away. Ministry requires activity, of course, but it also requires study.

Studying is personal. When it comes to lesson preparation, each minister should do his own study. This does not mean that the preacher has to "re-invent the wheel" each Sunday. All of us use resources (books, commentaries, podcasts, etc.), and we need to read widely and listen carefully to helpful sources. Even when I have an idea that I am convinced is completely original, chances are good that several others have thought of it before me. The issue is not whether I use sources, but how I will use sources. We need to be active in the lives of people in our congregation, but we also need dedicated time for our personal stories in order for ministry to mature.

MATURITY IN MINISTRY WELCOMES PERSONALITY WITHOUT BEING BASED ON PERSONALITY.

We need to understand ourselves. This is more difficult than it sounds because we don't often think carefully about how we function. During the spring of 2020, when COVID caused all of us to change our routines and deal with some challenges we had not previously faced, I was reminded that I am routine-oriented. In an era when office hours and worship schedules were changing, and there was no handbook on exactly how to handle everything, I felt lost. I had to develop and adjust to a new weekly routine.

If I want to accomplish my work efficiently during the week, it would be helpful to ask myself some questions. What time of day is easier for me to do my deep study of the text? Is it better to attack sermon preparation in the morning when I am fresh, or is it easier for me to find quiet time in the afternoon to study? When is the best time for me to accomplish administrative tasks, like e-mails and phone calls? How can I budget my time so that I can get those tasks done without spreading them throughout the entire day? Have you given thought as to how you work best and how you can structure a schedule to take advantage of that knowledge? Abraham Kuruvilla put it this way: "Someone once said that the three best friends of a sermon preparer are custom, habit, and routine."[3]

Another aspect of understanding ourselves is being honest with our own humanity. This can be tough, especially if you tend towards perfectionism (as I do). Admitting we have made mistakes and being willing to learn from them can be tough. It is important to remember that we gain credibility when we are honest about our own shortcomings. People need to know and understand we are human, not separated from the challenges of real life and the ability to make mistakes. In ministry, my goal is to take my service seriously, but not to take myself too seriously.

After all, my ministry is ultimately not about me, and I don't want to get in the way of the message. I have had the chance to travel to some of the Biblical sites in Israel on a couple of occasions, and as a result, I have witnessed incredible scenic views. At one of our stops, we visited the Herodium, the site of a palace built by Herod on a hill. When we arrived at the top, there was a beautiful view of the landscape below. I thought I would take a selfie, with my head in the corner, that I could send to my wife. I tried several times, but due to my lack of photography skills, I could not get a picture with my face in it where the entire scene behind me was visible. I kept taking up too much of the photo. I finally just turned around to get a great shot of the beautiful vista.

This experience reminded me of the challenge ministers face when serving in a church context. While our goal in ministry is to glorify God, we can often allow ourselves to get in the way. Transparency is important because we want people to know we are only human, which means we need to be willing to share stories from our own lives. Yet we want to be careful that our sermons don't contain so many personal updates and anecdotes that we become the focus of a lesson rather than God's Word. A mature ministry embraces our uniquely God-given personality but is not based on it.

MATURITY IN MINISTRY INCLUDES REMAINING TEACHABLE WHILE STAYING CONSISTENT.

To keep leading, I need to keep growing. If you preach or teach regularly, you understand the feeling of looking back at a sermon or lesson you wrote several years ago. That can be a humbling experience. Often, I immediately think of things I wish I had presented differently. The older I get, the more thankful I become for patient Christians.

I need to be willing to learn from all kinds of people. In Acts 18, Apollos had made a name for himself as an educated man, well-versed in the Law of Moses, and a talented speaker. Yet he was teaching an incomplete gospel. He only knew about the baptism of John, but he did not fully understand baptism into the name of Jesus. Aquila and Priscilla, Christians who were tent-makers by trade, took Apollos aside to teach him about Jesus. Not only is their initiative impressive, but the willingness of Apollos to listen to them is also noteworthy. Evidently, he did not consider his experience and eloquence as barriers to learning from two tradespeople.

It is often the case that ministers have the benefit of an education in ministry, and that can make it tempting for the minister to assume that he knows more about a given Biblical topic than others in a congregation. Of course, that is a dangerous (and usually mistaken) assumption. No matter the level of formal education, Christians who have spent years studying scripture and applying it to their life experience have a great deal to teach all of us. We are never beyond the need to be teachable.

Yet we also need to remain anchored in our core convictions. Trends come and go in every aspect of life, and ministry is no exception. There will often be ministry books, workshops, or seminars that will show how a new program or technique is causing congregations to grow rapidly. It is possible to start chasing the latest thing in church growth at the expense of our own faith foundation. We might find ourselves embracing strategies that don't have the proper theological grounding or that have negative implications we had not thought through earlier.

If we are going to lead in ministries, people need to have confidence that we will remain true to our foundation. In Ephesians 4:14, Paul discusses the importance of spiritual maturity, which he contrasts with life as a child, "tossed here and there by waves and carried about by every wind of doctrine, by the trickery of men, by craftiness in deceitful scheming ...." While we should always be teachable and growing in our faith, our ministry should also inspire confidence in others that we will steadily hold to our convictions about what matters most.

MATURITY IN MINISTRY EMBRACES HARD WORK BUT NOT UNREALISTIC EXPECTATIONS.

When it comes to ministry expectations, we are often operating between two extremes. One extreme would be that a preacher or minister is expected to be everywhere at every time and be involved in every ministry of a congregation. There may be some situations where it is possible for a minister to be involved with everything that is happening, but by and large that is not the case. Trying to keep up with a schedule that requires you to be everywhere and do everything can lead to burnout. There are loving (and tactful) ways to communicate our own limitations to members of our congregation.

We also do not need to burden ourselves with our own unrealistic expectations. My high school band director liked to say, "There is no such thing as a perfect performance." No matter how many hours we invested in preparation and rehearsal, we would never be flawless. While there are some Sundays where I feel like the sermon goes better than other times, I have yet to preach a sermon where I don't immediately think of how I could have done it better as soon as I sit down.

This is true with other aspects of ministry as well. We can sometimes feel pressure to do everything in ministry perfectly, and it is important to learn to laugh at ourselves. Several years ago, I went to visit a friend of mine in the hospital. I tried to think of something that would make him smile. I remembered that he had a little, battery-powered dog that was motion-activated. He kept it in his office, and every time someone came near, the dog would laugh uncontrollably and roll over. My sons were young at the time – ages 5 and 2, and they loved that little thing. So, I took it with me to the hospital and told him I had brought him some company. Once I showed it to him, he laughed and laughed. Then I set it down. After a long discussion, he and his wife asked if I would lead a prayer and I agreed. I began my prayer, and then I took one step forward, toward them. It was only then that I realized I had never turned off the motion-activated sensors. I didn't really know how to turn it off, so we just had to wait it out while we all laughed! We are imperfect, and we are going to make mistakes. We should not have unrealistic expectations.

Yet there is another extreme to avoid. In an effort to avoid the pressure to be everywhere and do everything, it could be possible to think that ministry should never be inconvenient or require more of me than I might feel able to give on a specific day. This attitude prompts me to think there should never be anything in my job description that I don't want to do. Someone could say:

> "I'm not really a people person, so I shouldn't be expected to talk to a lot of people."

> "I have never really enjoyed studying, so I shouldn't have to do much of that in my lesson preparation."

"I'm not an elder, so I shouldn't have to visit the hospital."

Maturity requires us to embrace elements of our role as ministers that we might not have chosen, but that need to be accomplished. We worship with Christians each Sunday who have jobs that require them to do at least one or two things they don't always feel like doing or that are out of their comfort zone. Not every aspect of their job descriptions comes naturally. Why should I expect something different? Ministry should not include unrealistic expectations, but it does require hard work.

Maturity in ministry does not come easily, and it certainly does not happen overnight. As I reflect on how I have observed these principles in the lives of effective ministers around me, I am encouraged to continue to grow in each of these areas.

ENDNOTES

[1] This essay is based on material originally presented as part of the 2023 Freed-Hardeman University Church Leaders Workshop.

[2] Jack Lewis, *Leadership Questions Confronting the Church* (Nashville, TN: Christian Communication, 1985), 103.

[3] Abraham Kuruvilla, *A Manual for Preaching: The Journey from Text to Sermon* (Grand Rapids, MI: Baker Academic, 2019), 11.

You Can Be a Leader, Too

JAMIE COX

Many times leaders are considered to be those holding esteemed jobs and positions (kings, presidents, and other rulers), but leaders are often ordinary, everyday people who guide others by their example. A father and his son walk along the beach. The boy stretches to place his smaller footprints in the impressions left by his father. No one tells him to do so; his actions come naturally. So does the follower walk after the leader?

Christ encourages those who follow Him to be more than just followers. He expects each disciple to be like Him. He expects us to recognize our role as leaders. Paul stated the concept when he instructed the Corinthians, "Now I commend you because you remember me in everything and maintain the traditions even as I delivered them to you" (1 Cor 11:1). "And what you have heard from me in the presence of many witnesses entrust to faithful men, who will be able to teach others also" (2 Tim 2:2). Not everyone can be a public leader, but all can be leaders in their own ways. Many examples throughout the Bible drive this point home. In fact, the Bible is filled with people whose examples lead us even today.

We can let Jonathan be our leader as we follow his lead of protecting a wrongly treated friend. Although Jonathan was the son of King Saul, he was still a young man when his father set out to kill David. As a young man, he showed tremendous loyalty to his best friend. Jonathan defied the king and risked his life when he shot the arrows, protecting David from the wrath of King Saul (1 Sam 20). We can follow Jonathan in defending right, whether in the church, family, or government.

We need to be a leader as Naomi was. Ruth left her country, friends, family, and gods to follow Naomi (Ruth 1:16). We often talk about Ruth's faith and sacrifice, but do we wonder why Ruth acted as she did? Naomi's example and leadership caused Ruth to accept the one true God as her God. Ruth took care of her mother-in-law, an aged and grieving woman, but ultimately, Naomi was as great a blessing to Ruth as Ruth was to Naomi.

We can let Esther be our leader and follow her example in protecting an entire nation from destruction. Although she became a queen, Esther was first an orphan, a woman, and a foreigner. Nothing in her early life showed her how to be a leader. The first chapter of the book of Esther dramatically shows the lack of respect and honor for women in her time. Despite her apparent limitations, God raised her to greatness. Through her obedience to God, she protected the Jews from slaughter by Haman. Even as a queen, Esther faced limitations, and only through courage and wisdom did she bring Haman to justice and counter his evil plot.

We can let Barnabas be our leader as we follow his example in giving our possessions to the Lord to help other Christians. Barnabas, "which means son of encouragement," was proof that the man fit the name by his selfless actions described in Acts 4. The encouragement that Barnabas showed in the earliest days of the church set the stage for even greater service. The Lord used him to help Paul become the great evangelist and apostle to the Gentiles.

Mary the mother of Jesus was not a public leader, but her life was so outstanding that God chose her to bear His Son. We can follow her example of purity, faith, and thoughtfulness. We can follow her example as a parent. We can ask ourselves the great question, "Am I living a life that would allow God to choose me to parent His only begotten Son?"

Christ is the ultimate leader. He, alone, left heaven for us. He, alone, died for us. No one loves us as the Lord does. He left us the ultimate example (1 Pet 2:21, Eph 4:11–16). In His love and wisdom, He has surrounded us with countless other examples of good. Even more, He calls us to serve as examples to this world and lead others to follow Him.

This article was originally printed in *Gospel Advocate* 146.8 (August 2004).

The Night Eternity Stood Still

KIRK BROTHERS

It was the night eternity stood still. Everything hung in the balance. Every event in human history led to this one moment in time. The co-creator of the universe, God the Son, lay on His face in an olive grove just east of the city of Jerusalem. Three of His closest friends slept a few feet away while Jesus poured out a broken heart to God. The hounds of hell licked their chops in anticipation and looked up at His misery with glee. The hosts of heaven looked down in sorrow as the Christ, the King of kings and Lord of lords, turned the dust of that lonely hillside into mud with His tears. Sweat poured from His body like blood from an open wound and mingled with the tears that flowed down His cheeks. It was an ironic foreshadowing of the moment which would occur the next day when a Roman spear point would bring forth from the Savior's side a mingling of water and blood. The Hebrew writer described the scene as follows: "In the days of His flesh, He offered up both prayers and supplications with loud crying and tears to the One able to save Him from death..." (Heb 5:7, all Scripture quotations are from the New American Standard Update).

THE CURSE OF FORESIGHT

David Roper observes, "When we behold Jesus in the garden, we see a side of Him seldom revealed in the Gospel record: the vulnerability of His manhood" (2003, 445). Jesus was aware that, in just a few mimutes, His enemies would arrive to arrest Him. He was cursed with the foresight of knowing what was coming: bonds, beatings, betrayal, a sleepless night, mocking, lies, condemnation, humiliation, brutality, and death. Within a few hours, a Roman scourge would tear the flesh from His body. The people He came to save, the people who lined the streets a week before to proclaim Him king, would demand His death. Soldiers would drive stakes into his hands and feet. He would struggle for every breath. No position would relieve the pain or the shame. His enemies would laugh as their spittle runs down the Savior's face.

Satan and the forces of hell would seem to have won. Jesus would be surrounded by humanity at its worst. Maybe the greatest pain came in knowing that the Father would—the Father must—turn His back on the Son. Though sinless, Jesus would be treated as a sinner. He would bear the sins of the world. The prophet, Isaiah, stated, "But your iniquities have made a separation between you and your God, And your sins have hidden His face from you so that He does not hear" (Isa 59:2). The sins of the human race would cause the Father to turn His face away. For the first time in all eternity, God, the Father, would not communicate with God, the Son. Maybe that is why Jesus wept?!

THE CHALLENGE OF CHOICE

He did not have to go through with it. The Father would not force Him to go to the cross. It was His choice. Maybe the words recorded in John 10:18 came flooding back into His mind:

> No one has taken it away from Me, but I lay it down on My own initiative. I have authority to lay it down, and I have authority to take it up again. This commandment I received from My Father.

Now was the time to decide. The forces of evil were mobilized. A detachment of soldiers was on the way to arrest Him at this very moment. It was now or never. What would he do? "Father, if You are willing, remove this cup from Me..." (Luke 22:42).

What did the angels think? Did they understand what was taking place? How much did they know? Peter referred to the Old Testament prophets by stating,

> It was revealed to them that they were not serving themselves, but you, in these things which now have been announced to you through those who preached the gospel to you by the Holy Spirit sent from heaven—things into which angels long to look (1 Pet 1:12).

There were things revealed to human beings which had not been made known to angels. Did the angels feel sadness at His sorrow? Did they quiver in righteous indignation when the soldiers struck their Commander in that garden? "Don't they know who that is?" or "How dare you strike the Holy One of Israel!", they may have thought.

The servant of Elisha awoke to find horses and chariots of the army of Aram (Syria) surrounding the city of Dothan. Elisha reminded his servant, "Those who are with us are more than those who are with them" (2 Kgs 6:16). The servant must have been puzzled as he heard this and looked around to see no army there to help them. But with eyes opened by Elisha's prayer, the servant suddenly saw the army of the Lord, horses, and chariots of fire, surrounding the army of Aram. Maybe that same army surrounded the Mount of Olives that fateful night when the Messiah prayed in agony. Jesus himself told Peter, "Or do you think that I cannot appeal to My Father, and He will at once put at My disposal more than twelve legions of angels?" (Matt 26:53). A legion represented the largest division in the Roman Army and estimates range in size from 3,000 to 6,000 men. Even the devil knew the angels would take care of the Christ. During the temptations of Jesus, Satan quoted Psalm 91:11–12:

> HE WILL COMMAND HIS ANGELS CONCERNING YOU; AND ON THEIR HANDS THEY WILL BEAR YOU UP, SO THAT YOU WILL NOT STRIKE YOUR FOOT AGAINST A STONE (Matt 4:6).

THE CALL UNHEARD

Seventy thousand angels stood ready to defend the Lord of Hosts. Two angels annihilated Sodom and Gomorrah. A single angel released the apostles in Acts 5 and a single angel released Peter in Acts 12. It would have taken only one angel to achieve victory in that small garden in Palestine. In my mind, I picture row upon row of angels encircling that small mountain. Did they ride blazing chariots and steeds that snorted fire? I picture each soldier in the angelic army gazing intently at the events in that olive grove. I imagine fiery horses pawing the night air in anticipation. What were the angels thinking? "Say it. Call us to your side. Just a nod from you and we will come swooping down upon this petty mob, end your misery, and take you back to the eternal glory that is rightfully yours!"

The Son never called for His legions and the Father only sent a single solitary soldier: "Now an angel from heaven appeared to Him, strengthening Him. And being in agony He was praying very fervently…" (Luke 22:43-44a). This lone heavenly messenger was not there to conquer or defend, but to comfort and strengthen. Humanity's only hope lay in a cross. If that angel had defended Jesus, the Lord would have received what He deserved but humanity could not have received what they desperately needed. It was not a defended Savior that they needed, but a dead One. Only by the death and resurrection of the Messiah could mankind have eternal life (Rom 5:6-11). The Son must be separated from the Father so lost humanity could be united with Him. Thus, the angel that stepped forth from the army of the Lord did not bear a sword, but a comforting touch. What did he say to Jesus? Did he speak at all? We will never know the answers to these questions on this side of eternity. We only know that our Savior suffered for us that night. We know that He had a pain that only Heaven could heal. We know that the Father cared about the Son's pain but could send no more than a single angel. To do more would mean disaster, the death of the scheme of redemption.

CONCLUSION

It was the night eternity stood still. I believe that on that fateful night, the hounds of hell and the hosts of heaven gazed on a small garden in Judea filled with gnarled olive trees, three slumbering servants, and a suffering Savior. We see the human frailty of the Lord in that Garden as a single angel came to comfort Him. We also see His Divine strength and courage as He lifted His head, dried His eyes, and marched to face his attackers: "Whom do you seek?" "Jesus the Nazarene." "I am He" (cf. John 18:4–5). Though He has the power to call forth the legions to defend Him, the Lord stays His hand. His enemies bind that hand and Jesus walks into history as the Savior of the world. The greatest expression of love may not be found in what Jesus did on the cross but in what He did not do in the garden. He did not call for the angels. He left His army behind and faced Satan's best, alone, the night eternity stood still!

WORKS CITED

Roper, David. *The Life of Christ, 2: A Supplement*. Truth for Today Commentary Series. Searcy, AR: Resource Publications, 2001.

Holy Bible: New American Standard Bible. 1995 edition. Lockman Foundation.

Scripture Index

Old Testament
Genesis
24:3	42	3:1–11	42
24:37	42	16:31	42
28:1	42	**2 Kings**	
Exodus		6:16	123
19:5	6	**2 Chronicles**	
20:8–11	5	8:11	42
34:21	5	**Ezra**	
Leviticus		9:12	42
19:18	57	10:14	42
24:8–9	6	10:44	42
Deuteronomy		**Esther**	
7:1–4	42	1	118
23:25	5	**Psalms**	
Joshua		1	28
23:12	42	91:11–12	123
Judges		119	28
3:6	42	**Proverbs**	
14:3	42	1:3	91
Ruth		1:10–19	93
1:16	118	1:15	93
1 Samuel		1:20–33	85, 87
20	118	1:20–23	87–88
21:1–6	6	1:24	93
1 Kings		1:24–25	93

1:24–30	89	4:5–7	30
1:25	93	4:6	123
1:26–27	89	4:17	29
1:28–32	90–91	4:18–22	29
1:31–32	91	4:20	35
1:33	92	4:23	29
2:13	93	4:23–25	30
2:15	93	4:25	35
2:18	93	5	50
2:20	93	5:16	58
3:13–18	93	5:17–20	17
3:17	93	5:21	30
4:6	93	5:27	30
4:14	93	5:31	30
5:5	93	5:33	30
7:25	93	5:38	30
7:27	93	5:38–40	53
8:5	93	5:38–48	49–50
8:20	93	5:43	30, 57
9:6	93	6:14–15	31
8:34–35	86	7:12	58
25:22	48	7:28	35
Isaiah		8:1–13	31
59:2	121	8:10–12	30
Daniel		8:18–22	30
7:13	10	8:27	36
Hosea		8:37	36
6:6		9:1–7	30
Micah		9:3	36
6:6–8	18	9:8	36
		9:8–13	30
New Testament		9:12–13	9
Matthew		9:22	30
2:16	95	9:29	30
3:13–17	28	9:33	36
3:15	28	9:34	36
4:1–11	28	9:36	30

10:1–32	29	20:20–23	36
10:18–23	30	20:20–28	98
10:24–25	38	21:1–11	35
11:1–3	36	21:23–27	31, 36
11:14	36	21:45–48	36
12:1	4	22:15–18	36
12:1–8	14, 20	22:16–22	31
12:1–14	18, 24	22:23–32	36
12:7	8	22:23–33	31
12:12	11, 20	22:34–36	36
12:22–37	31	22:39	57
12:22–30	20	23	9
12:24	36	23:2	17
12:27	20	23:13	30
12:38	36	23:23	7
12:38–41	31	23:31	20
12:38–45	31	26:6–13	36
12:47–50	28	26:14–15	36
13:10–13	31	26:31–35	37
13:52–58	36	26:36–46	37
13:53–58	30	26:39	99
15:1–2	36	26:53	123
15:1–9	31	26:56	35
15:3–6	5	28:17	37
15:28	30	28:18	37
15:30–31	36	28:18–20	34
16:1	36	**Mark**	
16:4	31	1:1–11	28
16:16	36	2:1	3
16:22	36	2:1–3:6	14, 23
17:24	36	2:1–12	3
18:21–35	31	2:10	12
19:1	36	2:13–17	3
19:1–9	31	2:14	12
19:6	20	2:17	9, 12
19:7	36	2:18–22	3
19:19	57	2:19	12

2:21–22	4, 12	15:32–42	98
2:23	4	16:15–16	34
2:23–28	1, 3, 15, 20, 23, 25	**Luke**	
		2:47	28
2:24	4	2:49	28
2:25		2:51	28
2:25–26	7	2:52	28
2:25–27	6	4:13	28–29
2:26	6	4:16–25	31
2:27	11	4:31–32	29
2:28	10–11, 15, 20	5:13	32
		5:31–32	9
3:1–6	3, 31	6:1	4
3:3–5	12	6:1–5	14
3:4	7	6:40	38
3:6	3	7:36–50	9, 31–32
3:17	98	8:1–3	32
5:36	97	8:19–21	39
5:41	97	8:38–39	32
7:1–13	32	9:23–26	30
7:8	5	9:46–48	31
7:10	5	9:51–55	98
7:24–30	39–41	9:53	36
8:34	4, 102	10:27	57
9:2–8	97	10:30–37	32
10:8	20	10:38–42	40
10:17–22	30	17:12–19	32
10:35–40	98	19:1–10	32
10:38	98	19:10	35
10:39	99	19:45–48	32
12:26	2	22:42	99, 122
12:28–34	7	22:43–44a	124
12:31	57	22:47–52	50
12:33	57	22:51	50
12:37	35	22:54	50
12:41–44	32	22:63	50
14:36	99	23:9	31

23:34	31	**Acts**	
23:35	50	1:1	26
23:43	31, 43	1:7	33
29:20–26	32	2	38
John		2:1–9	33
1:1	27	2:36	37
1:42	98	2:38	34
2	39	3:1–10	60
2:1–11	28	4	119
4	72	4:29–30	59
4:1–42	32	5	124
4:39	72	5:15–16	60
6:15	36	7	72
6:22–27	30	7:22	87
6:52	36	7:54–60	33
6:60	36	8:6–8	60
6:66	30, 35	9	34
8	40, 72	9:6	34
8:1–11	31	9:39	61
8:1–12	32	10:1–2	61
8:7	40	10:38	26
8:27	35	12	95–97, 99, 105, 124
10:7	30	12:2	99
10:9	30	12:4	96
10:18	122	12:15	96
11:16	36	12:23	96
13:1–11	31	13:5	1
13:1–17	50	14:8–10	60
13:1–20	32	18	112
13:8	36	19:11–12	60
14:2b–3	35	22:16	34
18:4–5	125	23:11	34
18:19–21	31	25–26	96
19:15	35	28:8–9	60
19:25–27	28	**Romans**	
20:27–30	37	1:8–13	34
21:15–20	32		

3:12	21	4:16	20
5:6–11	124	5:14	58
7:4	20	5:22–23	53–54
7:12	20–21	6:10	54
8:28	97	**Ephesians**	
8:34	35	4:11–16	119
11:17–24	61	4:14	113
11:18	61	4:29–32	54
12:1–2	48	5:25	43
12:14–21	48	5:27	35
12:17–21	49	5:28–30	57
12:20	48, 64	**Philippians**	
13:2	20	2:5ff	27
13.8–10	57	2.9–11	37
1 Corinthians		2:15	58
3:7	20–21	**Colossians**	
6:11	61	2	67
7:38	20–21	2:13	67
9:22–23	63	2:20	67
10:31–33	63	3:1	67, 70
11:1	117	3:12–13	53, 71
11:27	20–21	3:14–15	71
13:3	58	3:16	70
14:22	20–21	3:17	27, 74
15:29	20	3:18–21	67
15:58	26	3:18–4:6	67
2 Corinthians		3:20	67
1:3–4	35	3:21	67
4:12	20	3:22–23	70
5:16f	20	3:22–25	70
5:21	17	3:23–24	27
Galatians		4:1	71
2:10	61	4:2–3	71
3:9	20–21	4:5–6	64, 73
3:24	20	**1 Timothy**	
4:4	6	2:1–4	59
4:7	20	2:4	39

2:9–15	43	3:5	17
2 Timothy		**Revelation**	
2:2	117	1:5	37
Titus		2–3	34
2:7	26		
2:14	26		
3:1	27		
3:8	27		
3:14	27		
Hebrews			
2:17	63		
4:15	17		
5:7	120–121		
7:25	35		
7:26	17		
10:24	29		
11:13	33		
11:35	101		
13:2	64		
James			
2:1–5	61–62		
2:8	58, 61–62		
2:10	6		
5:6	17		
1 Peter			
1:12	122		
2:12	64		
2:21	119		
2:21–22	35		
2:21–24	31		
2:22	17		
3:18	17		
5:13	1		
2 Peter			
3:1–9	33		
1 John			
2:6	66		

Credits

Select Scripture quotations are taken from the NEW AMERICAN STANDARD BIBLE®, copyright© 1960, 1962, 1963, 1968, 1971, 1972, 1973, 1975, 1977, 1995 by The Lockman Foundation. Used by permission.

Select Scripture quotations are taken from the NEW KING JAMES VERSION®. Copyright© 1982 by Thomas Nelson, Inc. Used by permission. All rights reserved.

Select Scripture quotations are taken from the NEW REVISED STANDARD VERSION BIBLE, copyright © 1989 National Council of the Churches of Christ in the United States of America. Used by permission. All rights reserved worldwide.

Select Scripture quotations are taken from the Holy Bible, New International Version®, NIV®. Copyright © 1973, 1978, 1984, 2011 by Biblica, Inc.™ Used by permission of

CREDITS

Zondervan. All rights reserved worldwide. www.zondervan.com The "NIV" and "New International Version" are trademarks registered in the United States Patent and Trademark Office by Biblica, Inc.®

Scripture quotations marked HCSB are been taken from the Holman Christian Standard Bible®, Copyright © 1999, 2000, 2002, 2003 by Holman Bible Publishers. Used by permission. Holman Christian Standard Bible®, Holman CSB®, and HCSB® are federally registered trademarks of Holman Bible Publishers.

Select scripture quotations are from The Authorized (King James) Version. Rights in the Authorized Version in the United Kingdom are vested in the Crown. Reproduced by permission of the Crown's patentee, Cambridge University Press.

Select scripture quotations are from the ESV® Bible (The Holy Bible, English Standard Version®), copyright © 2001 by Crossway, a publishing ministry of Good News Publishers. Used by permission. All rights reserved.

Select scripture quotations are from Revised Standard Version of the Bible, copyright © 1946, 1952, and 1971 National Council of the Churches of Christ in the United States of America. Used by permission. All rights reserved worldwide.

Scripture quotations marked (NLT) are taken from the Holy Bible, New Living Translation, copyright ©1996,

CREDITS

2004, 2015 by Tyndale House Foundation. Used by permission of Tyndale House Publishers, Carol Stream, Illinois 60188. All rights reserved.

Select scripture quotations are taken from the (NASB®) New American Standard Bible®, Copyright © 1960, 1971, 1977, 1995, 2020 by The Lockman Foundation. Used by permission. All rights reserved. www.lockman.org

Heritage Legacy Series

The Heritage Legacy Series follows the longstanding academic tradition of the *festschrift*, a collection of essays in recognition of a respected colleague. Biblically, it embodies the principles of giving honor to whom honor is due and esteeming godly servants for their work. Heritage Christian University Press is happy to show appreciation to those who have blessed Heritage Christian University and the church in countless ways.

Things Most Surely Believed: Festschrift for Charlie Wayne Kilpatrick. Heritage Legacy Series. Edited by the Staff of Heritage Christian University Press. Florence, AL: Heritage Christian University Press, 2021.

Serving the Lord: A Festschrift for Freddie Patrick Moon and Janet Stewart Moon. Heritage Legacy Series. Edited by the Staff of Heritage Christian University Press. Florence, AL: Heritage Christian University Press, 2022.

Fighting the Good Fight: A Festschrift for Bill Bagents. Heritage Legacy Series. Edited by the Staff of Heritage Christian University Press. Florence, AL: Heritage Christian University Press, 2022.

A Gentle and Quiet Spirit: A Festschrift for Barbara A. Dillon. Heritage Legacy Series. Edited by the Staff of Heritage Christian University Press. Florence, AL: Heritage Christian University Press, 2023.

Do All in His Name: A Festschrift for Mechelle Thompson. Heritage Legacy Series. Edited by the Staff of Heritage Christian University Press. Florence, AL: Heritage Christian University Press, 2024.

Also by Heritage Christian University Press

Redrawing the Blueprints for the Early Church: Historical Ecclesiology in and around the Stone-Campbell Movement by John Young

Berean Study Series. Edited by Ed Gallagher and Bill Bagents

Clothed in Christ: A How to Guide

Cloud of Witnesses: Ancient Stories of Faith

The Ekklesia of Christ: Becoming the People of God

For the Glory of God: Christ and the Church in Ephesians

Instructions for Living: The Ten Commandments

Led By God's Spirit: A Practical Study of Galatians 5:22–26

Majesty and Mercy: God Through the Eyes of Isaiah

Visions of Grace: Stories from Scripture

What Real Christianity Looks Like: A Study on the Parables

Cypress Bible Study Series. By Ed Gallagher

The Book of Exodus: Explorations in Christian Theology

The Gospel of Luke: Explorations in Christian Scripture

The Sermon on the Mount: Explorations in Christian Practice

Heritage Christian Leadership Institute Series

Corrupt Communication: Myths at Target Church Leaders
by Bill Bagents and Laura S. Bagents

Counseling for Church Leaders: A Practical Guide
by Bill Bagents and Rosemary Snodgrass

Lead Like the Lord: Lessons in Leadership from Jesus
by W. Kirk Brothers

Heritage Legacy Series. Edited by the Staff of Heritage Christian University Press.

Do All in His Name: A Festschrift for Mechelle Thompson

Fighting the Good Fight: A Festschrift for Bill Bagents

A Gentle and Quiet Spirit: A Festschrift for Barbara A. Dillon

Serving the Lord: A Festschrift for Freddie Patrick Moon and Janet Stewart Moon

Things Most Surely Believed: Festschrift for Charlie Wayne Kilpatrick

To see full catalog of Heritage Christian University Press and its imprint Cypress Publications, visit www.hcu.edu/publications.

www.ingramcontent.com/pod-product-compliance
Lightning Source LLC
Chambersburg PA
CBHW050241010526
44107CB00040B/1472/J